AF277746

Color in Knitting:

By Designers, for Designers

Anna Gitelson-Kahn
Jörg Hartmann

arnoldsche

Contents

Foreword

My first experiences in knitting were as a teenager in the textile workshop of the family factory, where in the evening I could find some hand knitting machines to use. By following the brief and necessary instructions by some of the workers on the evening shift, I was able to satisfy my curiosity about how these machines could actually produce those special and imaginative sweaters that my parents created, and which I, too, had been wearing for a few years.

The machine that I found free most often was an 8-gauge machine whose needles were large enough for me to see how they moved. I took a reel of yarn dyed in a nice color, and after threading it through the various eyelets all the way to the yarn feeder, slowly moving the carriage by hand, I watched with growing curiosity the movement of the needles as they slid up to "chew" it. They were sliding up and down, crossing over each other and tying the yarn with their hooked heads. Needle after needle, stitch after stitch, the carriage moved one way and then the other, row by row. Little by little my beautiful colored yarn was turning into a colored knitted fabric, almost like magic. A yarn of color became a three-dimensional element, a colored material structure, a surface where color was gathering with depth and dimension.

Learning about the possibilities of needle use, I tried different effects of alternating work on the front and on the back beds, doing ribs, racking, or loosening or tightening the stitch. With the diversified use of needles, it was possible to create an even more complex material structure, on both tactile and visual levels.

Working with a 5-gauge machine, therefore with larger needles, by doubling the threads I was using, I could create the same things and the same structures but obtain an even more material result with an optical dimension of greater relief and perception. It was almost a magnifying-glass effect that made the knotted structure, of which knit is made, more perceptible. Even the color in this case was more dynamic, taking on more body and depth. The showy materiality had, for me, a great exploratory charm.

I could change not only the color but also the type of yarn, simply by replacing the cone. Thus the structure of the knitwear varied in a linear way but also in its chromatic component, by using yarns of different colors. Fil-à-fil, stripes, rifling, barré: by alternating material and color in succession, I experimented with sequences that were both material and chromatic at the same time, waiting in anticipation to see that colorful knit coming out of the machine that would make me want to wear it.

Over the years the technological development of machines to produce knit fabric has allowed it to spread incredibly far, even to sectors not strictly related to clothing. The fact remains that knitwear in all its expressions is the material medium where color can be revitalized and enhanced with that great versatility that allows us to wear it freely on our bodies and also to be able to cover and furnish the spaces in which we live.

Luca Missoni

Preface

There are many beautiful, inspiring, and engaging books that explore the various aspects of knitwear, including its history, design processes, and technology. It is for this reason that we chose to narrow our scope in order to provide a thorough examination of the use of color. *Color in Knitting: By Designers, for Designers* invites you to journey through the world of color in knitwear design and to discover its limitless potential. The book is focused exclusively on the subject of color in relation to flatbed technology, excluding other key knitting methods, such as shaping techniques, that are not directly related to designing with color. As a result, we hope this book serves as a valuable resource for designing with colors in flatbed knitting.

Color has been a crucial element of knitting design from the earliest days. The Stoll historic sample archive, which dates back to its founding in 1873, offers a glimpse into the manifestation of colors over the past 150 years. Examining the archive, we can see how color aesthetics have evolved alongside technological advances from the earliest mechanical machines to the latest electronic machines and CAD systems.

Now, designers can create unique and surprising color interactions, blending hues in ways that were previously unimaginable. From mixing secondary colors from primary ones, to changing the intensity of colors, to fading them out, the possibilities are endless.

I clearly remember a conversation I once had with a retailer. He told me that, for him, knitwear represents a way to add color to his product assortment. He said his buying strategy for woven apparel is usually based on classic, neutral colors like blue shades and natural hues. However, with knitwear, he is willing to take more risks and incorporate current color trends into his stores selection.

Color trends are just one of many factors that influence designers' use of color, along with fashion trends, novel fibers, spinning methods, and dyeing techniques. Yet innovations in flatbed knitting machines and software have profoundly impacted the color of knitted textiles. These advancements have provided designers with new and exciting ways to unleash their creativity and to experiment with color—as well as to bring their designs to life more quickly.

Years ago, I stood next to a flatbed knitting machine, experimenting with different yarn cones and colors to create jacquard and intarsia patterns. The speed at which I could see the results of my color choices was impressive—it only took a few minutes to change the cones and see the effects on the finished panel. The set-up time was in stark contrast to that of other textile techniques, like weaving or circular knitting, which can be exponentially more time-consuming. This is one reason why flatbed knitting is such a powerful tool for creating beautiful and unique designs: it allows designers to quickly and easily refine their color combinations and to experiment with different variations.

Nowadays, designers can experiment with color virtually for faster, more efficient, and sustainable color exploration. However, the technical features of flatbed knitting technology play a crucial role in the final color appearance for a given garment or accessory. When designers are familiar with all options available to them, they have the full array of tools to create stunning and appealing color combinations in their knitwear. The book is not meant to provide a complete overview of every possible combination and technique but rather a foundation and resource for your future designs.

We are grateful to have the support of Anna Gitelson-Kahn, Associate Professor and Graduate Program Director of the Textiles Department at the Rhode Island School of Design, in cowriting this book and ensuring its suitability for use in education. We hope that *Color in Knitting: By Designers, for Designers* will inspire and empower you to unleash the emotional potential of color in your knitwear creations.

Jörg Hartmann

How to Use This Book

front and
rear needles

knit
(front) stitch

knit
(rear) stitch

weft yarn

front-rear stitch
(full rib)

float

front tuck

rear tuck

front to rear
transfer

rear to front
transfer

front needle
cast-off

rear needle
cast-off

Every knitted fabric is made of yarn; every yarn has a color, even an undyed one. Yet, our perception of the color of a knitted fabric is heavily influenced by the knitting structure as well as by the yarn's characteristics.

This book's journey begins when two yarns of different colors come together to create a knit (polychromatic knitting). In *Color in Knitting: By Designers, for Designers,* we focus on methods of constructing multicolor knits, including knitting structures, techniques, and technologies. Other color-related finishes, like dyeing, printing, or embroidery, we chose to not discuss to keep our focus narrow.

In the first section of this book, we have selected samples from past decades that we believe best illustrate the different methods of multicolor knitting and the resulting color effects. The photographs of samples emphasize the appearance of the color and texture, rather than the shape of the sample. Some samples also include the reverse side to show how techniques impact both sides of the fabric. All knitting structures and techniques depicted apply to all types of apparel fabric or technical textiles, such as automotive or furniture upholstery, shoe uppers, medical applications, or architecture.

Next to the samples, you will find keywords that represent the specific structures and techniques used in the creation process. These keywords can help you navigate between the samples and the technical chapters. Additionally, each sample is accompanied by a Stoll Patternshop code, so you can find it online (https://patternshop.stoll.com) to learn more details about it, including shape construction, machine gauge, knitting time, and yarns. From there, you can download high-resolution copyright-free photos as well as knitting programs. The samples are intended to inspire further developments as well as to be used directly as they are.

The second part consists of technical chapters that provide insight into the specific structures and techniques used to create the samples previously presented. Our goal in this section is to provide you with a technical foundation, so you may further explore and manipulate the described structures and techniques to achieve your own goals when combining colors in knitting.

This part includes stitch notations (diagrams) written using basic knitting symbols to further illustrate the construction of a knit. Diagrams consist of technical rows; each one equivalent to one single knitting system action, such as the passage of a yarn in a stitch formation or additionally required needle actions (e.g., transfers or stitch cast-off). Multiple technical rows might be needed to form one knitted row of a knitting structure. Diagrams are read from the bottom up, similar to the way knitting is formed on a machine. Symbols of stitch notations include front bed and rear bed needles, yarn, knit (front) stitch, purl (rear or back) stitch, front-rear stitch (full rib), float, front tuck, rear tuck, front to rear transfer, rear to front transfer, front needle cast-off, and rear needle cast-off.

To help you navigate these numerous samples, we compiled a matrix, found at the end of this book. It summarizes samples provided and connects them to the relevant technical chapters, allowing you to either start by looking at the samples and then exploring the technique behind them, or by starting with the technique and then finding the samples that employ it.

As we look to the future, it is clear that technological innovation is poised to bring even more excitement to the realm of multicolor knitting. Amidst constant evolution and advancement, the fundamental principles of knitting will remain unchanged. We believe that a thorough understanding of these principles can not only improve one's own work but also inspire and inform the development of new technology.

Color Journey

2310001

Color Journey

Precise Inverse Plating

Stripes   Intarsia   Precise Inverse Plating

Color Journey

1510063

Stripes   Intarsia   Cast-off Elongated Stitch

1810116

Stoll-ikat plating® Stoll-weave-in®

2110062

Stripes Intarsia Stoll-weave-in®

1710036

1510042

Cross-Tubular Jacquard   Precise Inverse Plating   Stoll-ikat plating®

Stoll-weave-in®

2210023

1210036

Stripes   Cast-off Elongated Stitch

1210181

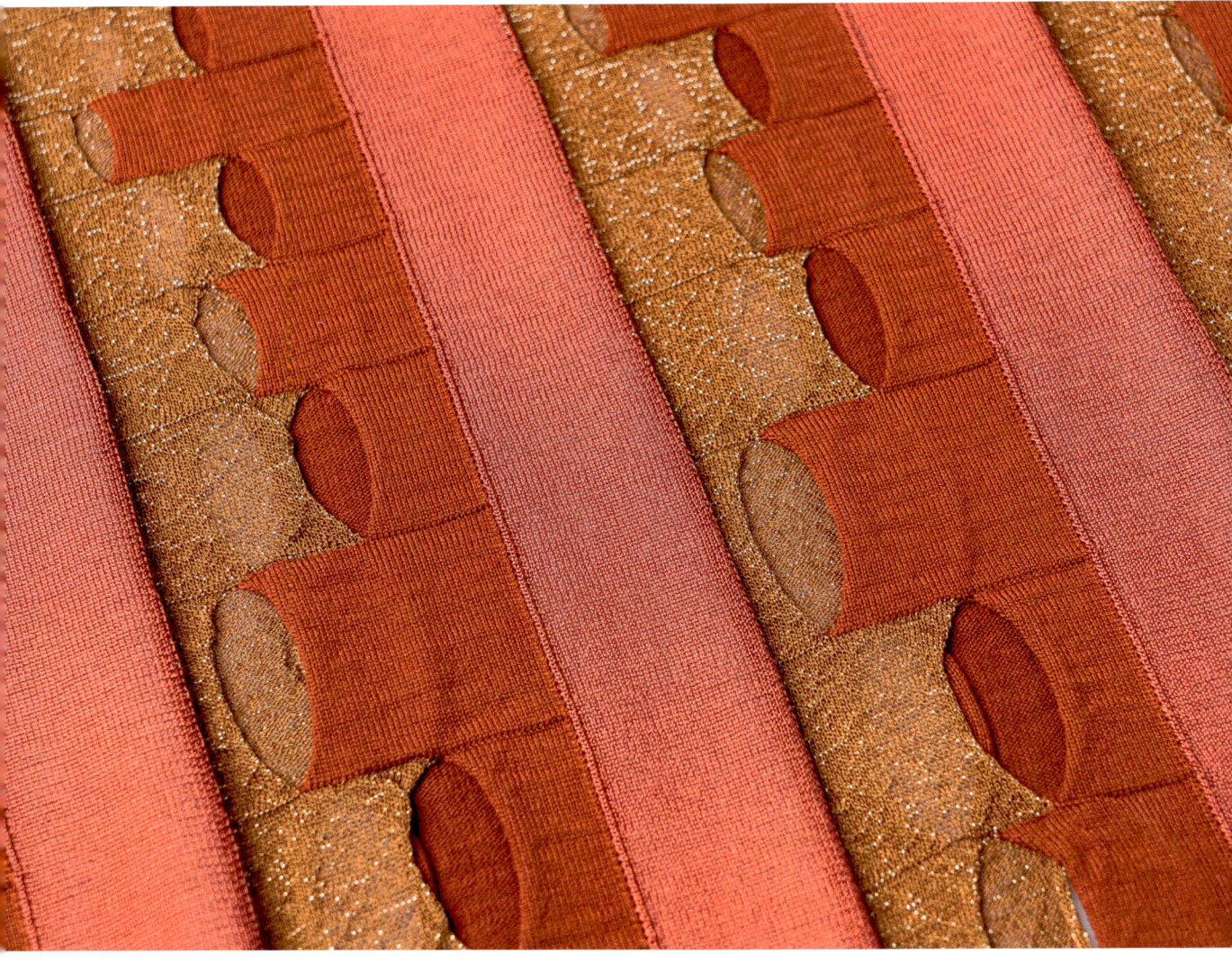

1210041

Intarsia

2210019

Color Journey

0810458

(Stripes) (Intarsia) (Cross-Tubular Jacquard)

1110385

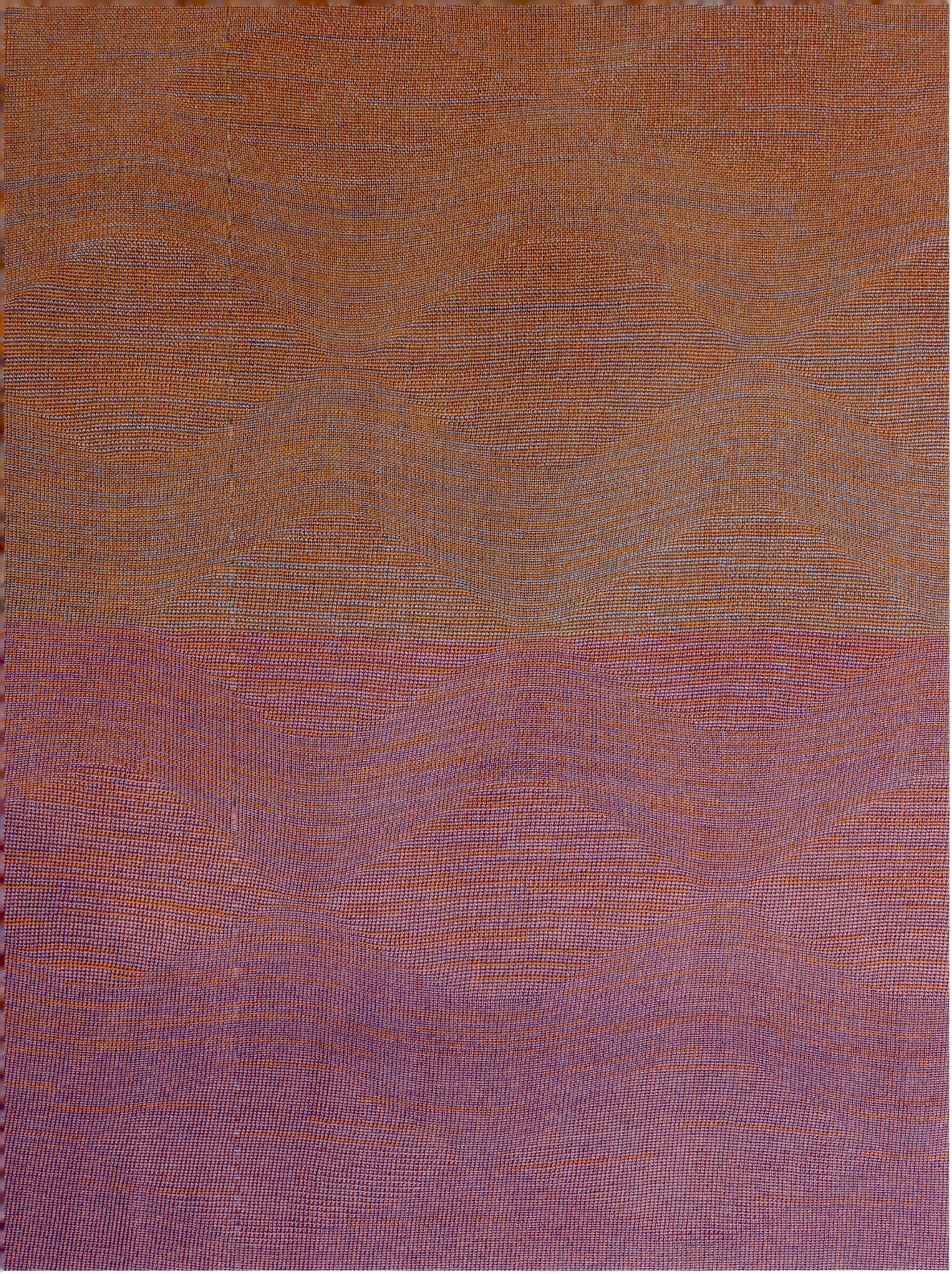

1410162

Stoll-ikat plating®

PTS Elongated Stitch

1410160

Intarsia   Stoll-ikat plating®

1210227　　(Intarsia)　(Traditional Plating)　(Cast-off Elongated Stitch)

2310002

Cast-off Elongated Stitch

1810051

Twill Jacquard   Net Jacquard   Stoll-weave-in®

1510044   Precise Inverse Plating   Stoll-weave-in®

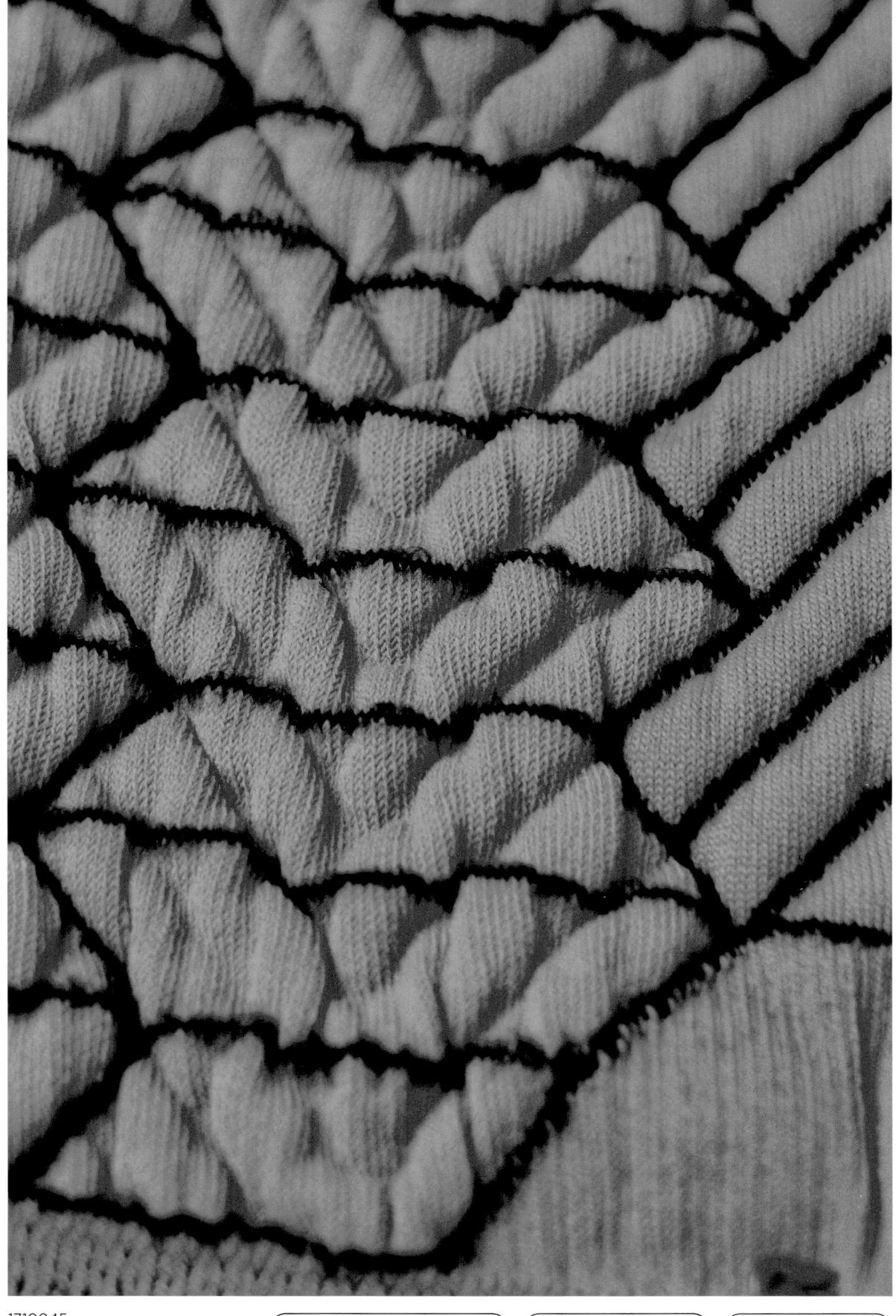

Cross-Tubular Jacquard   Stoll-ikat plating®   Stoll-weave-in®

1210144

Devoré

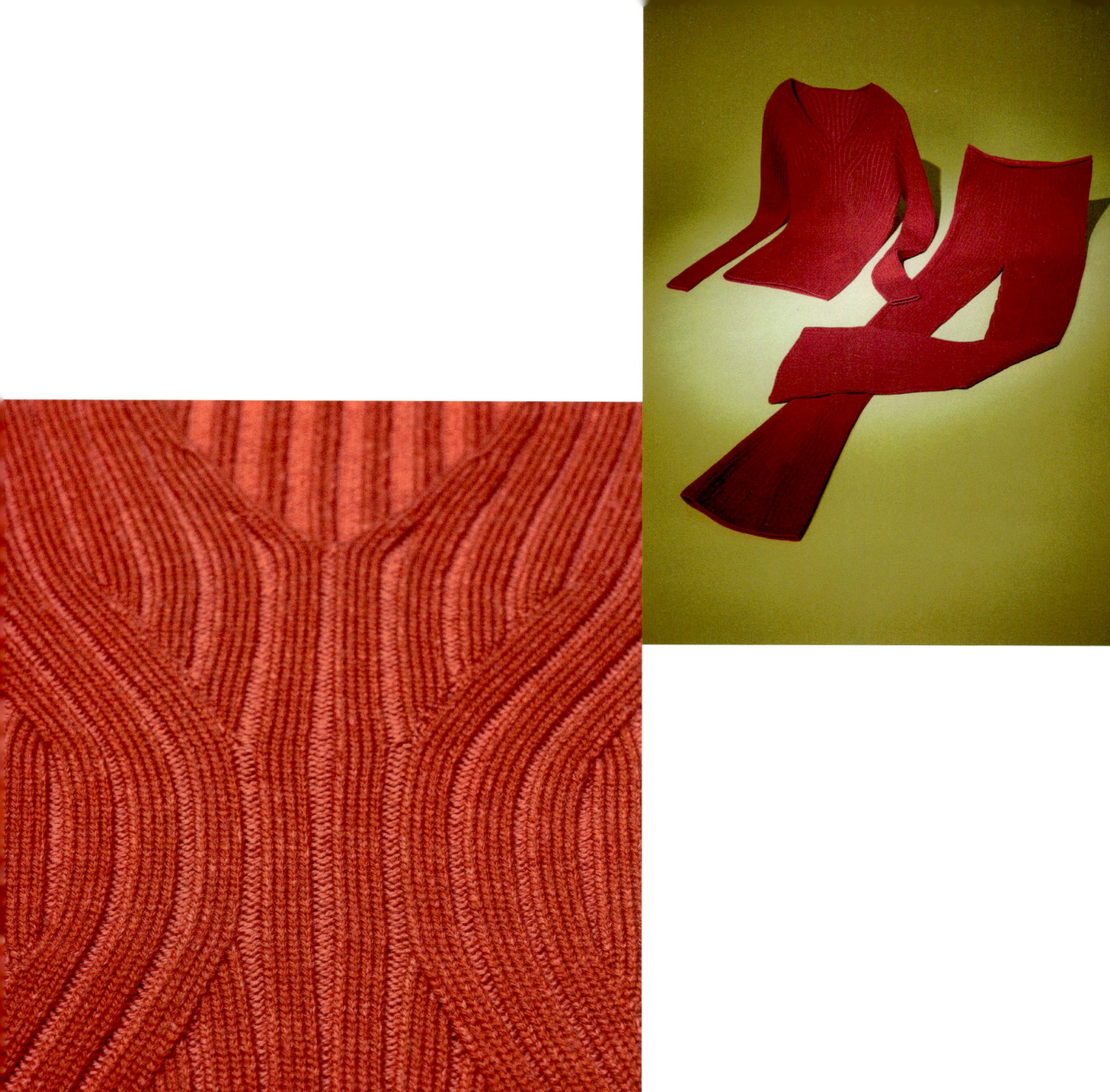

2310006

Traditional Plating

1210059

(Intarsia)

1210157

1510102

(Cross-Tubular Jacquard)   (Precise Inverse Plating)   (Stoll-ikat plating®)

(Stoll-weave-in®)

2210029

Traditional Plating

2210034

Stripes   Precise Inverse Plating

0610427 (Intarsia) (Twill Jacquard) (Cross-Tubular Jacquard) (Cast-off Elongated Stitch)

1910078

(Intarsia) (Traditional Plating)

(Selective Plating) (Stoll-weave-in®)

1910052

(Precise Inverse Plating)   (Stoll-ikat plating®)

(Stoll-weave-in®)

2110005

Selective Plating   Devoré

2110045

(Devoré)

2210039

(Twill Jacquard)

Stoll-ikat plating®   Stoll-weave-in®

2110058

(Stripes) (Intarsia) (Cross-Tubular Jacquard) (Precise Inverse Plating)

(Stoll-ikat plating®)

1610056

Cross-Tubular Jacquard

Stoll-ikat plating®

Float Jacquard   Selective Plating

2210027

Traditional Plating

Intarsia   Stripe Jacquard   Stoll-ikat plating®   Plush

1210021

Color Journey

Stripes   Intarsia

1210101

Intarsia   Cast-off Elongated Stitch

Stripes   Stoll-ikat plating®   Selective Plating   Stoll-weave-in®

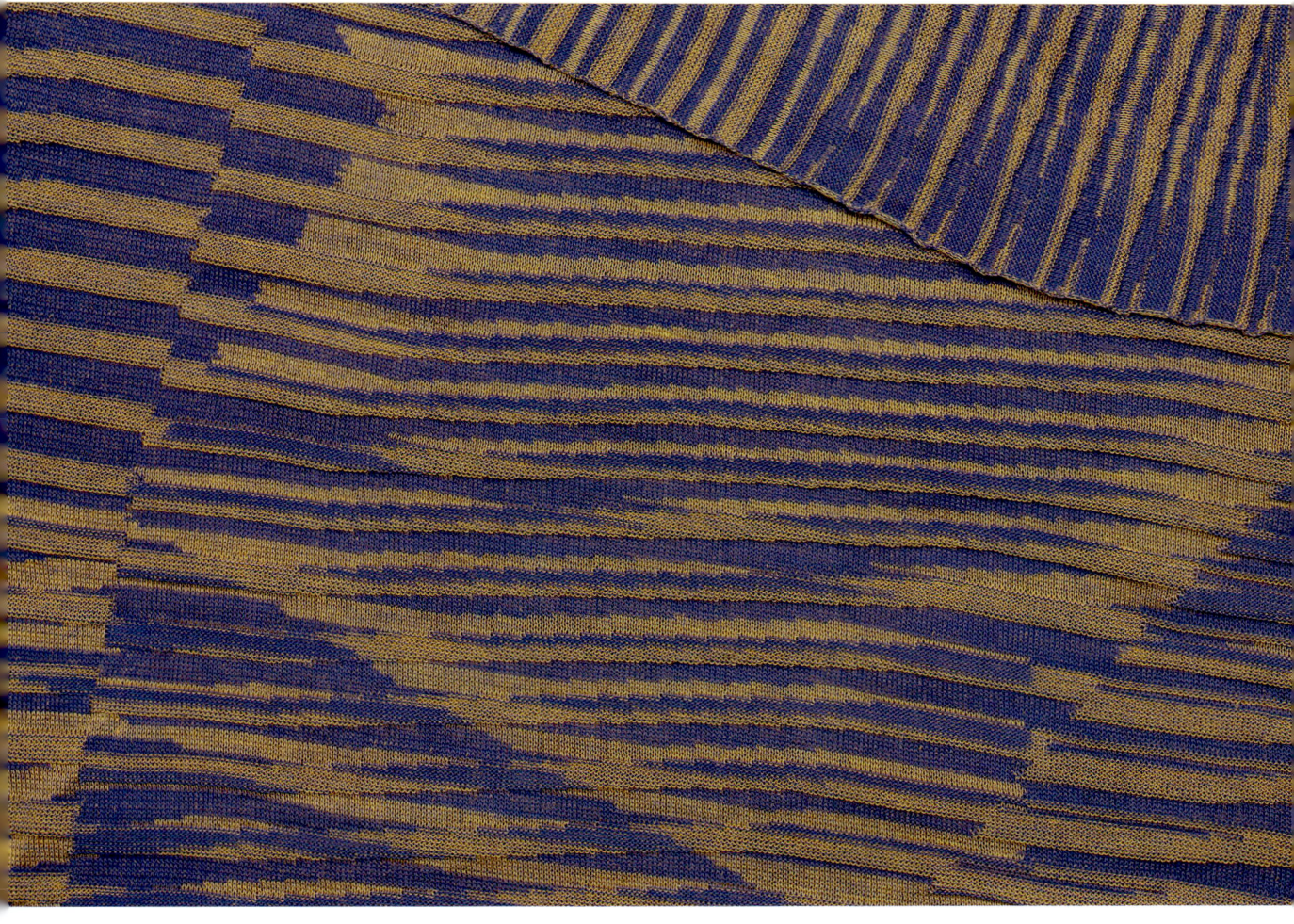

1410168

Stoll-ikat plating®

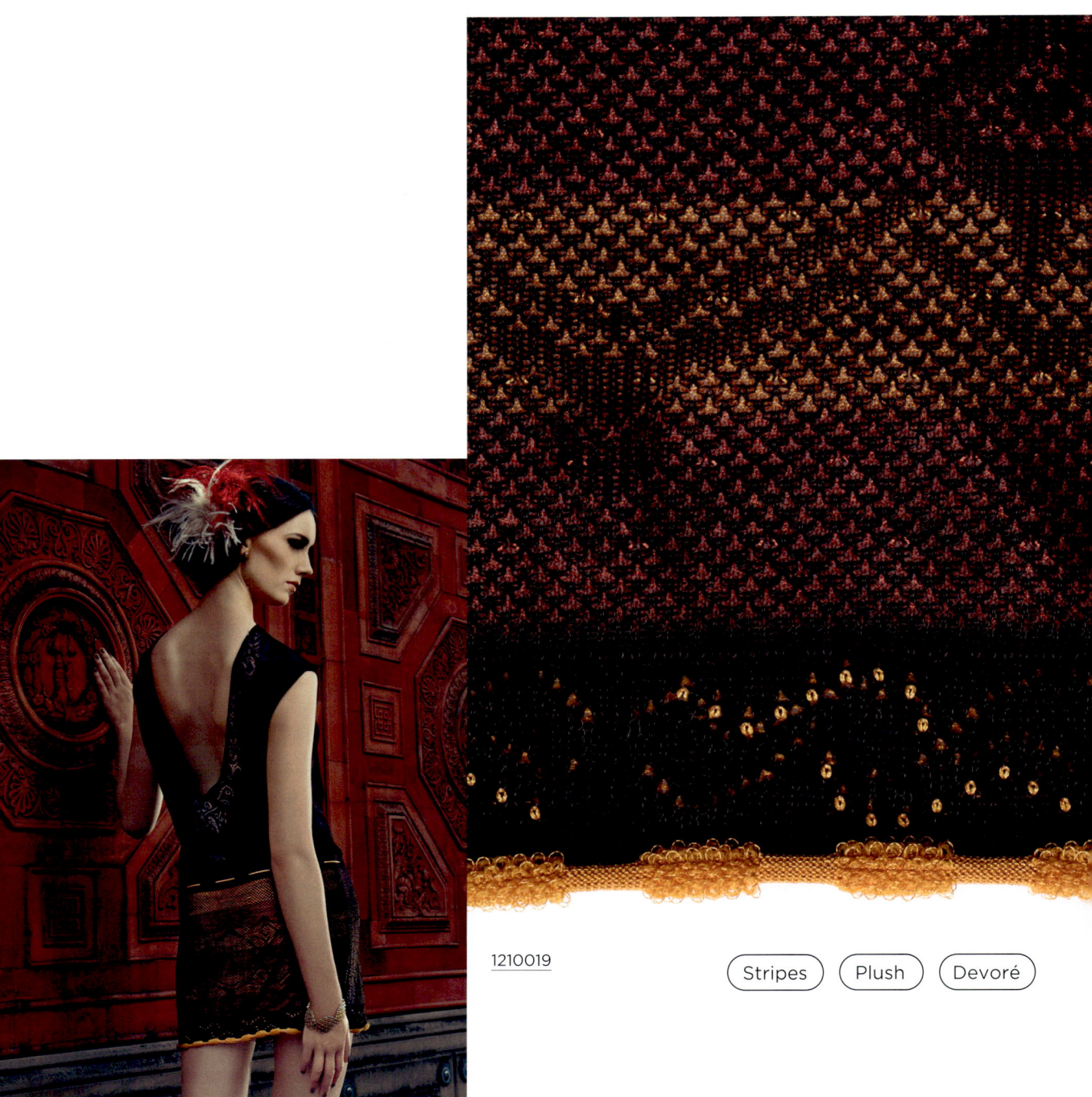

1210019

Stripes   Plush   Devoré

Intarsia   Cast-off Elongated Stitch

Twill Jacquard   Cross-Tubular Jacquard

Color Journey   **65**

2110073

(Cross-Tubular Jacquard) (Stoll-ikat plating®)

1710022

Intarsia Selective Plating

1510036

(Precise Inverse Plating)　(Stoll-ikat plating®)　(Stoll-weave-in®)

Cast-off Elongated Stitch

1410128

Color Journey

1410097

(Precise Inverse Plating) (Selective Plating)

1610003

(Cross-Tubular Jacquard) (Relief Jacquard) (Stoll-ikat plating®)

(PTS Elongated Stitch)

1910047

(Intarsia) (Precise Inverse Plating) (Selective Plating)

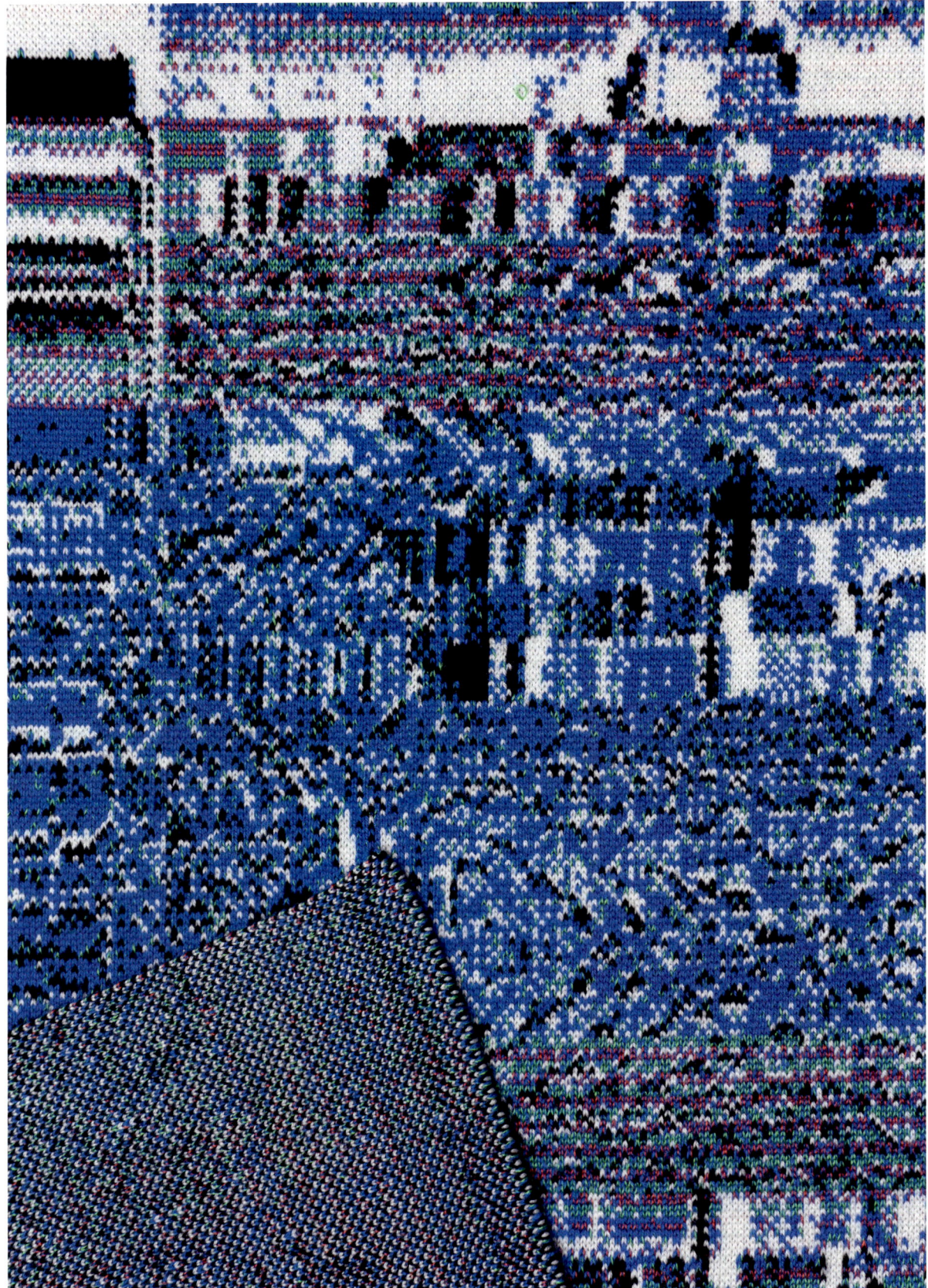

(Twill Jacquard)   (Stoll-ikat plating®)

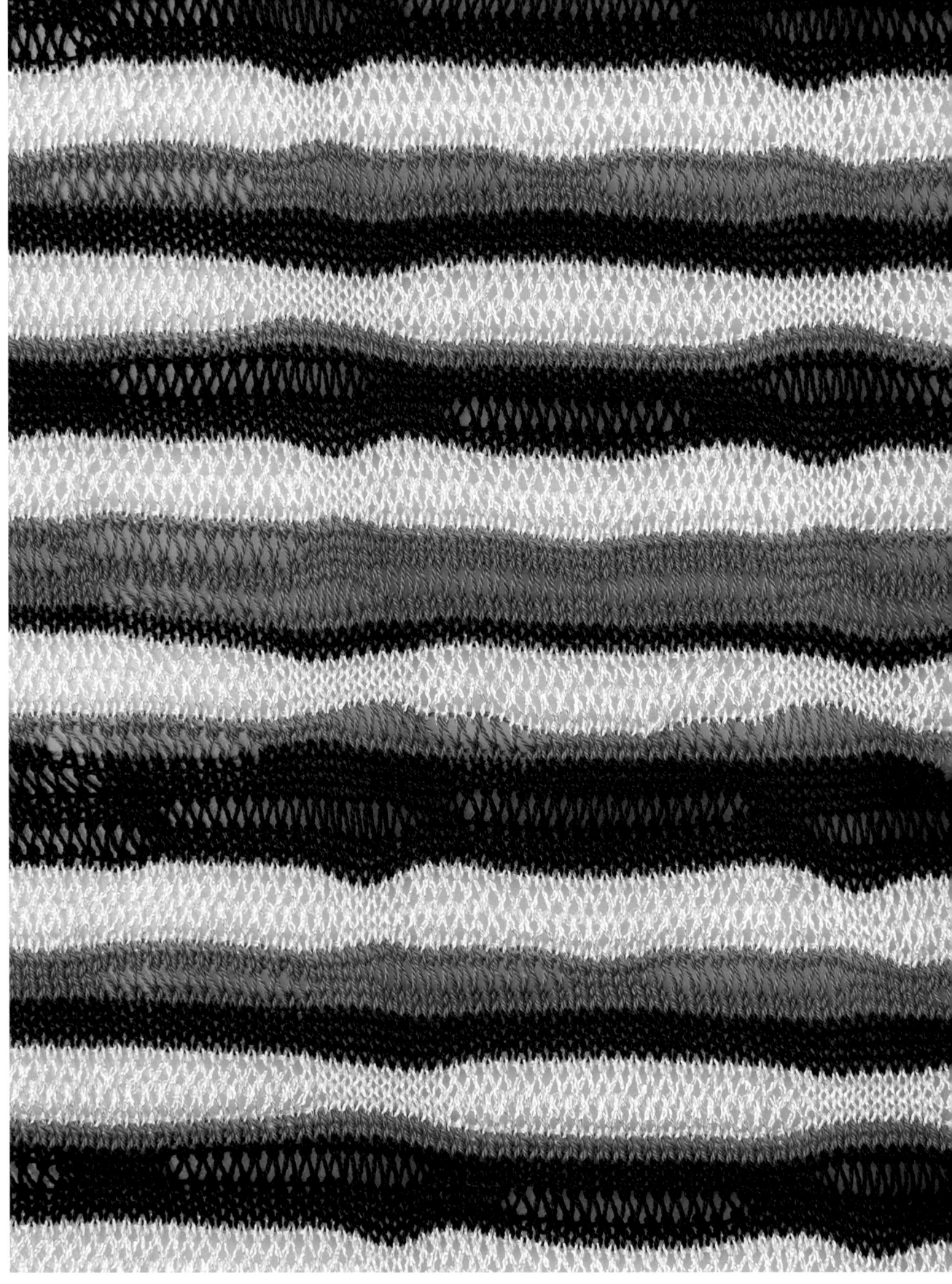

0810433

1410161

82 Color Journey

1410172

Stripes   Precise Inverse Plating   Stoll-ikat plating®   PTS Elongated Stitch

Color Journey

83

1210166

(Stripes) (Intarsia) (Float Jacquard)

1210177

(Stripes) (Traditional Plating)

1310018

Stripes   Float Jacquard

Traditional Plating

0510021

Intarsia

0710429

Cast-off Elongated Stitch

Intarsia   Stripe Jacquard

1310079

(Stripes) (Float Jacquard) (Precise Inverse Plating)

1910063

(Intarsia) (Traditional Plating) (Stoll-weave-in®)

Stripes   Cross-Tubular Jacquard   Stoll-ikat plating®   Stoll-weave-in®

1610053

(Stripes)　(Stoll-ikat plating®)

(Stoll-weave-in®)

1510002

(Stripes) (Precise Inverse Plating) (Stoll-ikat plating®)

Intarsia   Stoll-ikat plating®   Stoll-weave-in®

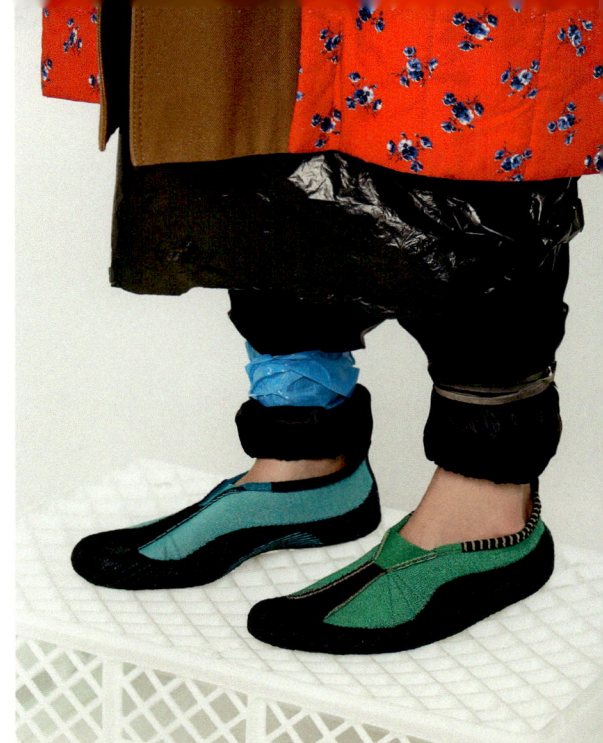

1810090

(Stripes) (Intarsia) (Cross-Tubular Jacquard) (Precise Inverse Plating)

(Selective Plating) (Stoll-weave-in®)

1810088

(Stripes) (Intarsia) (Stoll-ikat plating®)

(Stoll-weave-in®)

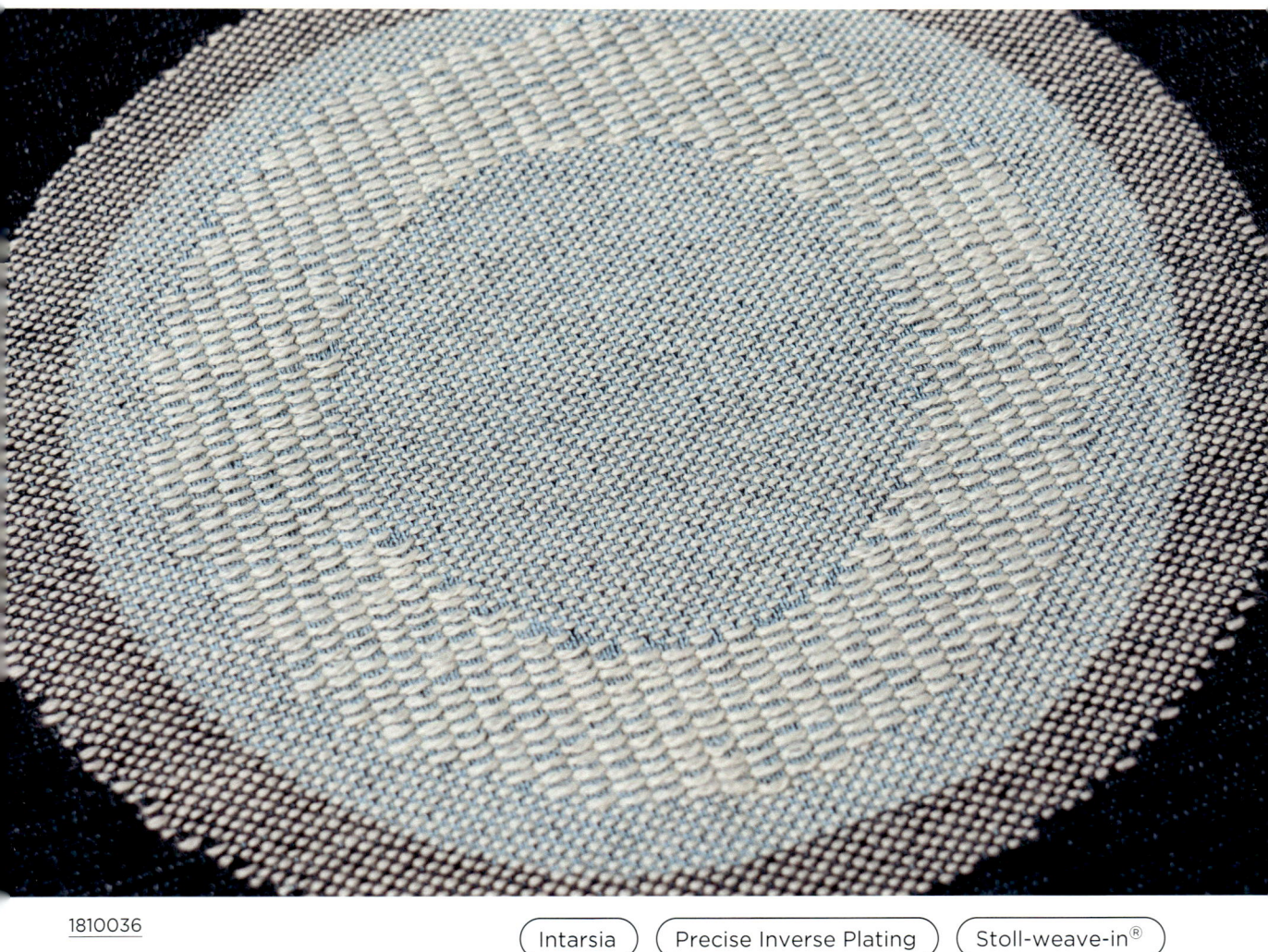

1810036

Intarsia · Precise Inverse Plating · Stoll-weave-in®

(Stripes) (Intarsia) (Stoll-ikat plating®) (Plush) (Stoll-weave-in®)

1910024

(Intarsia) (Random Plating)

(Stoll-ikat plating®) (Stoll-weave-in®)

2210026

(Intarsia)   (Traditional Plating)   (Stoll-ikat plating®)   (Stoll-weave-in®)

1910027

(Precise Inverse Plating) (Stoll-ikat plating®) (Stoll-weave-in®)

2110029

Stripes   Stoll-ikat plating®   Stoll-weave-in®

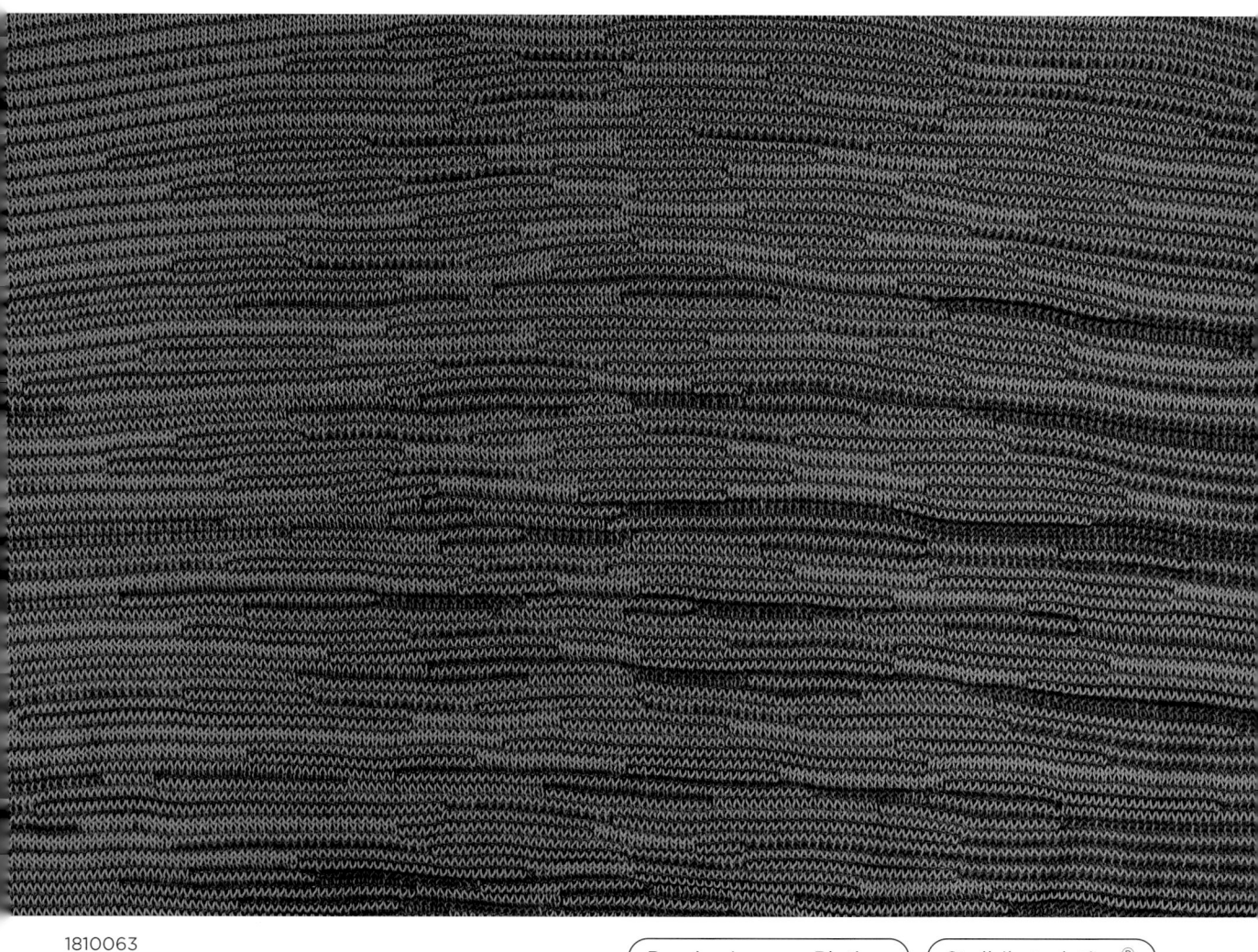

1810063

1910042

106   Color Journey

(Intarsia)   (Selective Plating)   (Devoré)

1010443

Stripes Cast-off Elongated Stitch

2110072

Stripes   Stoll-ikat plating®   Plush

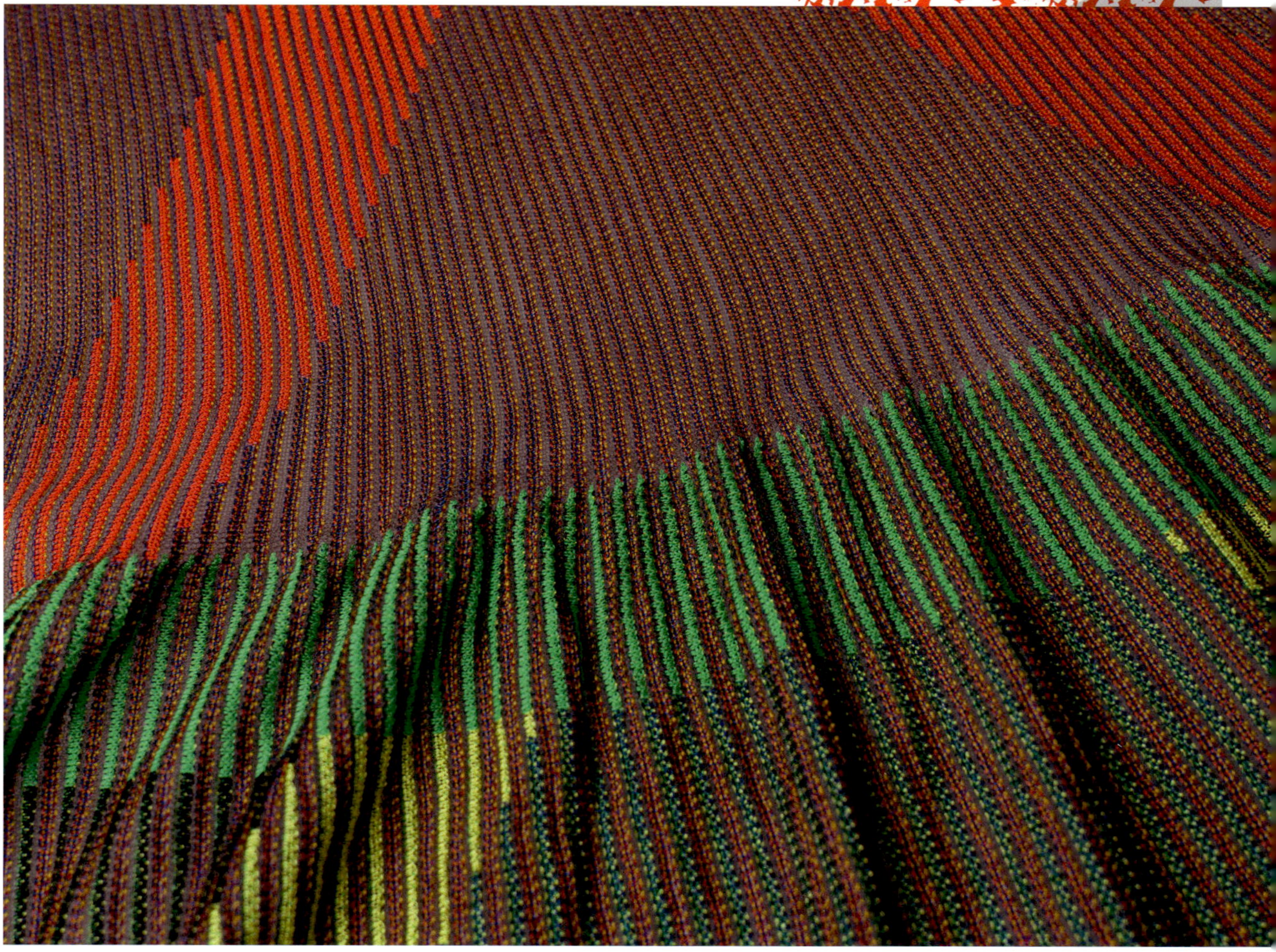

1510077

Stripes   Twill Jacquard

Stripes Float Jacquard PTS Elongated Stitch

110 Color Journey

1410117

(Stripes) (Cross-Tubular Jacquard)

(Relief Jacquard) (Traditional Plating)

Technology Overview

Stripes

Structure- independent color effect

Stripes are the simplest way to combine colors in a knit. Stripes can be bold and graphic, subtle and suggestive, or active or quiet, depending on the color combination and stripe proportions. Single- or double-row striping provides a great base for small-scale textural grid patterns, such as Milano rib variations and optical illusion effects, when combined with a full or half cardigan, or links-links (aka garter stitch) structures. Great color effects can be achieved with single row striping combined with Stoll-ikat plating® and elongated stitches (see chapter 5.0, Elongated Stitch, for details). Interesting zig-zag and undulating lines can be created by combining stripes with pointelle or racking. Stripes can run the full width of a fabric or appear only in selected areas when combined with intarsia or partial knitting.

Stripes

0810416

NOTES

Possible on any machine.

Multiple yarn qualities, counts, and effect yarns can be combined.

Can be combined with any knitting technique and structure.

ATTENTION

For smooth knitability, an even number of rows for stripes is recommended.

In a striped pattern, a color that is not knitted stays at the side of the fabric until it is used again, resulting in a vertical float at the side. The height of the stripes determines how long these side floats will be. The number of colors in a stripe pattern determines the number of floats at the selvage of the fabric.

0810454

0810408

Stripes

Intarsia

Structure-independent color effect

Intarsia is a multicolor method of knitting that allows the use of different yarns next to each other in the same row of knitting. Each yarn is threaded into a different yarn feeder and is knitted in a specific area determined by an artwork. This localized use of yarn feeders enables the creation of color patterning in lightweight single-jersey fabrics. The vertical borders between two knitted neighboring color fields can be closed or left open (fig. 1210059).

Since intarsia is structure-independent, it can be combined with any knitting structure. Fig. 0610427 shows intarsia used with both jacquard and pointelle. It also can be used with almost any knitting technology, such as plating, plush, or devoré, making intarsia an extremely versatile designing tool.

The number of different yarns that can be used in the same row is limited by the number of yarn feeders available, shown in fig. 1210059. In this example, 28 yarn feeders are used simultaneously to knit 28 different color fields within one row.

Intarsia works well with bold, geometric graphic imagery (fig. 1210059) but can be trickier for more detailed artwork. Fig. 0610281 and fig. 0510021 show clever ways of using intarsia to create intricate textural visuals; fig. 0610427 illustrates what can result when combining intarsia with jacquard.

Using intarsia for multicolor knitting results in stronger color saturation compared to other knitting structures and techniques like jacquard or plating (see chapters 3.0 Jacquard, and 4.0 Plating, for more details), in which other colors are always present and impact the color of the front despite being held at in the back of the fabric. Consequently, in intarsia the colors of the yarns are kept in their purest form. Intarsia further allows for true transparency when used with very fine or transparent yarn.

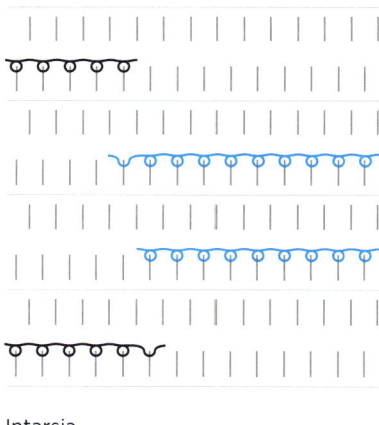

Intarsia

1210059

0610281

Intarsia

When considering the number of yarn feeders required for a particular artwork, it is important to distinguish between the number of colors and the number of color fields. For example, a black square on a white background is a two-color artwork that has three color fields, two for the white background on the right and left side of the square, and a black one for the square itself. It will require three yarn feeders to be knitted in intarsia.

Not all feeders of a machine will be available for knitting intarsia. On most machines, at least three yarn feeders will be assigned to technical yarns, like the separation thread (also termed draw thread), elastic comb thread, and protection yarn (also known as waste yarn). This will reduce the number of feeders available for intarsia.

Stoll ADF technology improves intarsia production time and quality as well as supporting more challenging artworks:

Colors can be added at any time with an ADF, as shown with the yellow square in fig. 1210059.

Color fields can be as narrow as 12.7 mm.

ATTENTION

Not every artwork is knitable in intarsia. Narrow color fields might be difficult to execute.

Artworks with curved shapes such as dots are less accurate than artworks with geometrical shapes, such as diamonds.

Using a larger number of colors will increase machine setup time.

Depending on the artwork, more color fields might lead to a longer finishing time to cut and sew-in all the yarns' ends.

Intarsia

Intarsia

Technology

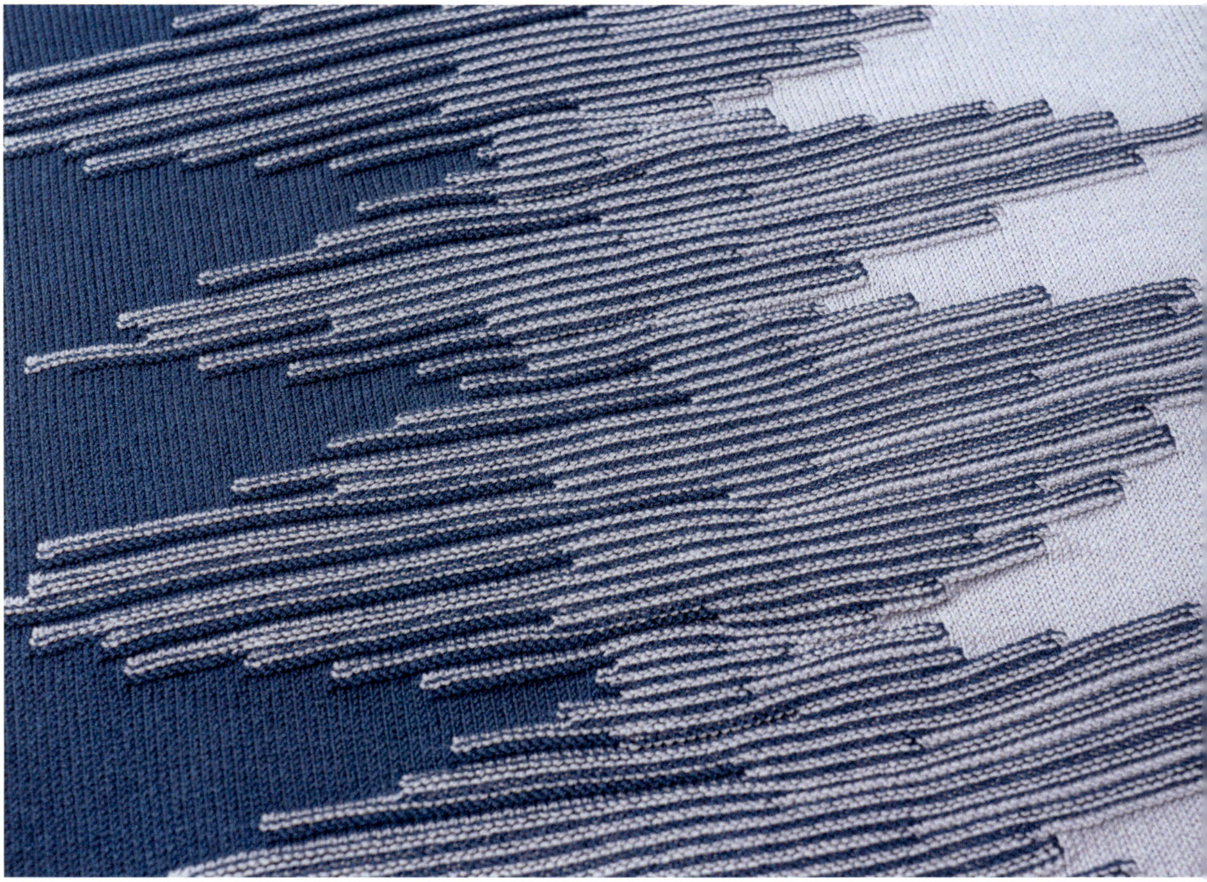

Jacquard

Structure-based color effect

Color jacquards, also known simply as jacquards, are a family of multicolor knitted structures based on individual needle selection that create color imagery on the face of a jacquard. Either side of the fabric can be the jacquard's face. The other side is referred to as the back. All colors used in one row of jacquard will be involved in a knitting structure of that row, in contrast to intarsia, where each color works independent of the others. In jacquards, while one active yarn or color is visible on the front of the jacquard, the other yarns are held at the back.

Most jacquard structures are double-bed structures, apart from float jacquard, which is the only one knitted on a single bed. Traditional jacquard types can be easily identified by the color patterns they create on a jacquard's back: float, stripe, twill, and net. Cross-tubular is an exception; its name refers to its knitted structure, and its back will show a negative image of its front.

All double-bed jacquards can have areas of single-bed knitting incorporated into a structure. Those areas are called reliefs. A relief will be visible on the face side of a jacquard, exposing a purl or the reverse side of a jersey, while the back will maintain a color pattern characteristic of its corresponding jacquard. The relief areas will be thinner and more see-through than the rest of the fabric. Further modifications of jacquards could be done by switching between the face and back sides of the jacquard, as shown in fig. 2210039, and by programming custom jacquards that combine and/or alter the classic jacquards mentioned above.

A jacquard structure can be placed over the entire fabric, in horizontal sections or in selected areas in combination with intarsia. Combinations with intarsia will be used to create areas of jacquard within other structures (fig. 0910622 in this chapter and fig. 0610427 in 2.0, Intarsia); they can also be used to introduce an additional yarn within a confined area of a jacquard, as in fig. 2110058.

There are no limits on imagery that can be knitted with jacquards; they can have repeated patterns or they can be engineered to have no repeat. Jacquards can have color details of any scale, including a single stitch. Color can be freely used all over the fabric and changed from one stitch to another anywhere within. Some limitations apply to artwork created for float jacquard; those are discussed in detail in the following subchapter.

The recommended number of colors per row varies from two to six colors and is dictated by the particular jacquard structure as well as the yarns' counts. The number of colors will affect both the visual and functional aspects of the knit. The more colors used in one row, the more distorted the imagery becomes, and the resulting fabric becomes more and more unbalanced, i.e., the face vs. back row counts will differ. The total number of colors used within the jacquard and defined by the artwork can be higher than six, as long as the number of colors used simultaneously is appropriate for the chosen jacquard structure. For instance, twelve-color artwork can be knitted in a three-color jacquard. If combined with plating, the number of colors can be expanded dramatically without altering the knitting structure (fig. 1310079).

By combining yarns of different thicknesses, dimensional and textural effects can be created in addition to a color effect. When a very fine yarn is used on the face of a jacquard, it will create see-through areas; all other yarns of the jacquard will show through, and their colors will optically mix together, a color effect similar to that of reliefs.

NOTES

There is no limitation on supported imagery, except for float jacquard (details in its subchapter).

Double-bed jacquards tend to be heavy compared to single-bed structures.

Double-bed jacquards also result in flat fabrics that do not roll at the edges, and have nice self-finished edges.

Color brilliancy will be affected by a chosen jacquard structure, discussed further below.

Different yarn counts can be used successfully together.

Double-bed jacquards can accommodate yarn thinner than required by the gauge of the machine.

ATTENTION

It is recommended to design artwork for jacquards over an even number of rows.

Depending on the jacquard type and number of colors used, the front and back row count might differ and will need to be balanced by adjusting stitch sizes. More details for each jacquard type are provided in the following subchapters.

The jacquard knitting structure as well as the number of colors used will distort the proportions of the original artwork's imagery That will require the artwork to be scaled (stretched up or shrunk down vertically) based on the stitch density of a test swatch.

For best results, the number of colors per row might be limited to six, depending on the structure.

Fully fashioned shaping with jacquards is time consuming. Using cut and sew or shaping at the selvage can be used to decrease the production time.

For thick yarns a smaller number of colors per row is recommended.

Combining jacquard and partial knitting will require careful programing.

Jacquard

Float Jacquard

Float jacquard, also known as single-jersey float jacquard and, in hand knitting, as Fair Isle knitting and stranded colorwork knitting, is a multicolor single-bed structure. To create a color pattern on the face of this jacquard, each yarn involved in a particular row of knitting knits on needles corresponding to its color field and floats over needles of other color fields. The stitch diagram below shows two different color yarns forming together one row of a two-color float jacquard. When one color is visible on the front, the other color floats behind it.

This structure works best with an artwork that consists of only two colors per row and has smaller-scale graphic elements with color fields that are ideally not wider than an intended machine gauge. For instance, color fields of no more than 7 stitches for a 7-gauge machine, 12 for a 12-gauge, etc. This limitation to artwork will keep floats on the back of the jacquard around or under an inch long, which makes them suitable for smooth knitting. Longer floats that do not meet these requirements can alternatively be tucked to the back of a fabric, but depending on the yarn choice, tucks might become visible on the face of the fabric.

Fig. 1310079 shows a Fair Isle-inspired two-color float jacquard with inverse plating and rows of purl stitches.

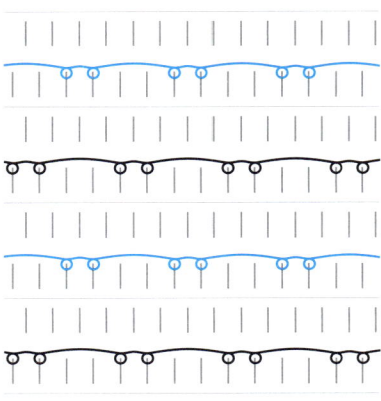

Two-color float jacquard

1310079

1010185

NOTES

Fabric will roll at the edges, similar to single-jersey knits.

Has the least elasticity of all jacquards. Floats limit horizontal fabric stretch.

Since the float jacquard structure uses only one bed, it can be easily used in layered knitting, such as tubular knitting, ottomans, flaps, integral knitting (Stoll-knit and wear®), etc.

Can be used with other single- and double-bed structures. For example, fig. 1010185 shows the back side of a four-color float jacquard combined with single-bed striping.

If longer floats are unavoidable, net jacquard might be considered as an alternative structure that has similar color brilliance but keeps floats length under control.

ATTENTION

Most effective with two colors.

Long floats might snag and get caught during knitting and may interfere with the wearability of a garment.

It is recommended to keep floats under one inch in length and to use color fields no wider than the machine gauge dictates (e.g. 7 stitches for a 7-gauge machine or 12 for a 12-gauge).

Jacquard

Twill Jacquard

Twill jacquard, also known as birds-eye jacquard or all needle jacquard, gets its name from its characteristic twill-like pattern on the reverse side. It is a double-bed structure where each color is knitted on both beds. Every color yarn is knitted on every needle of its color field on the face side, and on every other needle on the rear, independent of the color fields (see the stitch diagram below). The ratio between the number of rows created on the face of this jacquard to the number of rows created on its back is 1: (number of colors)/2. For example, for two colors, the ratio will be 1:1, since there will be one back row for each of the face rows; the fabric will be balanced and will eventually not require any stitch size adjustment. For six colors, the ratio will be 1:3 [1: (6/2)] and will need to be technically balanced by increasing the front stitch size and/or decreasing the back stitch size.

Fig. 1810034 shows a three-color twill jacquard with one of the yarns plated of two colors; the Stoll-ikat plating® method is employed to create a color glitching effect. As was mentioned before, the face and reverse of the jacquards can be combined on the same side of the fabric. The example in fig. 2210039 shows a three-color twill jacquard created in that way. It also shows the characteristic ghostly image of the face in the reversed areas.

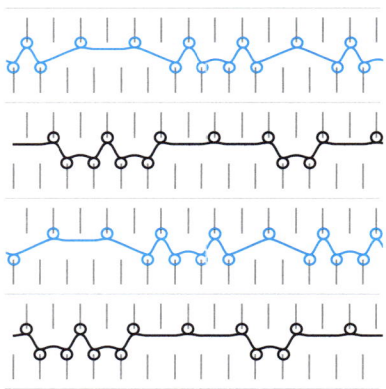

Two-color twill jacquard

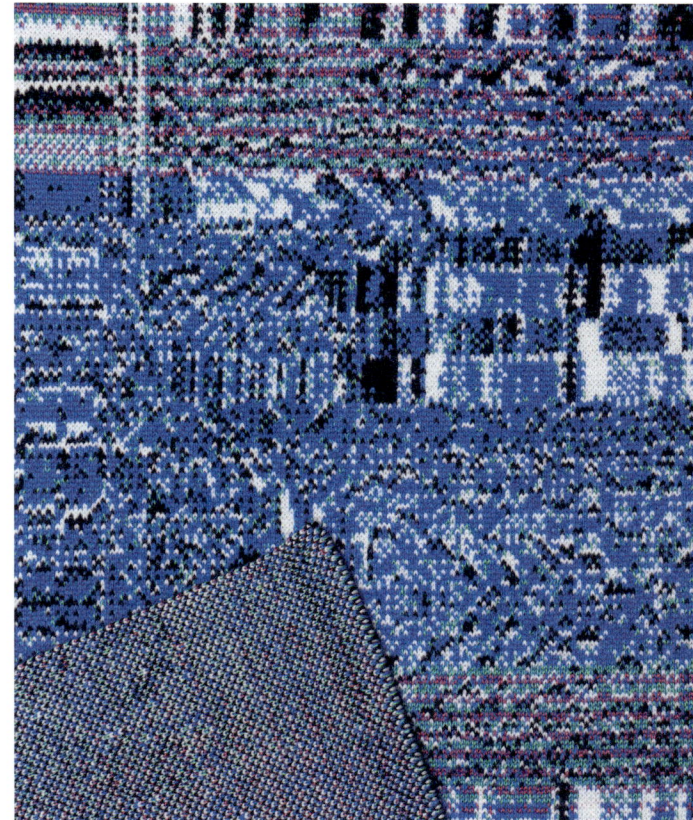

NOTES

Color brilliance is slightly compromised in comparison to cross-tubular or float jacquards.

Is dense with lower elasticity than single-bed structures. Twill jacquard will lay flat and not roll at the edges.

The ratio between the number of rows created on the face of this jacquard to the number of rows created on its back is 1: (number of colors)/2.

Unbalanced for number of colors greater than two and will require different stitch lengths for face and back to compensate.

The color pattern on the back is uniform but will have a slight ghost appearance of the face's image.

Jacquard

Stripe Jacquard

Stripe jacquard, also known as half Milano jacquard, full rib, or all needle jacquard, is characterized by a striped reverse side. Similar to twill jacquard, each color of the stripe jacquard is knitted on both beds with all needles knitted on the rear (see the stitch diagram). This means all colors of the face make a single row striping pattern on the back. The structure is unbalanced even for two colors; there will be two rows on the back of the jacquard for every row on the face. Stitches on the face side will appear longer than those on the back side and will let all the colors of the back show through. Compared to other jacquards, colors used in stripe jacquard will influence each other the most. The back side, in addition to striping, will have an image reminiscent of the one on the face, as shown in fig. 0910622.

Fig. 0910622 shows a two-color stripe jacquard knitted in intarsia and separated by cables knitted with an additional yarn.

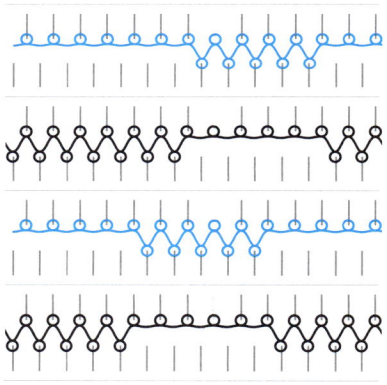

Two-color stripe jacquard

NOTES

Color brilliance is compromised by being able to see through the stretched stitches of the face.

Dense with lower elasticity than single-bed structures. Twill jacquard will lay flat and not roll at the edges

The ratio between the number of rows created on the face of this jacquard to the number of rows created on its back is 1: (number of colors).

The structure is unbalanced even for two colors and requires different stitch lengths for the face and back to compensate.

The color pattern on the back is uniform but will have a ghostly appearance of the face's image (fig. 0910622).

The most commercial jacquard with high production output.

Jacquard

Cross-Tubular Jacquard

A cross-tubular jacquard, also known as tubular or double jacquard, is based on the tubular knitting structure. Its construction is different to that of stripe and twill jacquards. Instead of knitting on both beds simultaneously, each color is knitted only on one. A yarn of one particular color is knitted only on the front within its color field, and on the back, outside of it (see the stitch diagram). This structure creates two layers that only connect at the vertical borders of color fields, when yarns are switching between beds, which gives the cross-tubular jacquard its name.

When only two colors are used, the fabric will have a reversed color image, a negative, of the face on its back. Out of all the double-bed jacquards, cross-tubular maintains the cleanest and most brilliant colors. For jacquards with more than two colors, the knitting of colors on the back will be done on every other needle and will resemble the look of twill jacquard but without the color uniformity. When used with two or three colors, the structure will remain balanced.

Fig. 2110058 shows a two-color cross-tubular jacquard with the background color blocked with the use of intarsia. In addition, the use of the Stoll-ikat plating technique® applied on both sides of the fabric (two colors on the front and two colors on the back) enriches the color range considerably.

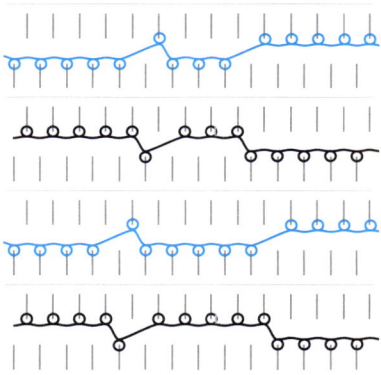

Two-color cross-tubular jacquard

NOTES

Color brilliance is maintained.

Elasticity is similar to single-bed structures, and will lay flat and will not roll at
the edges.

Fabric tends to be heavier and have a
higher yarn consumption than other
jacquards.

Fabric consists of two layers connected
through the image.

Ratio between the number of rows created on the face of this jacquard to the
number of rows created on its back is 1:1
for two or three colors, and 1: (number of
colors - 1)/2 for more than three colors.

Balanced, even for two or three colors.

Color pattern on the back of the fabric is
a reverse of the pattern on the front.

Often used with only two colors for full
reversibility.

2110058

Jacquard

Net Jacquard

Net jacquard, also known as ladder back jacquard or simply tubular or double jacquard, is a variation of cross-tubular jacquard with a lighter and open back side. Instead of knitting on all needles of the back, this jacquard can be knitted on every second needle for 1x1 net, or every third needle for 1x2 net, etc. The back layer will be more open and will show a net-like structure, giving this jacquard its name. The color pattern of the back will be similar to that of the cross-tubular jacquard. The lightness of the back of this jacquard makes it a great choice to be used with four or more colors and for heavier yarns. This jacquard tends to be voluminous due to its open net structure.

Fig. 1810051 shows a three-color 1x1 net jacquard.

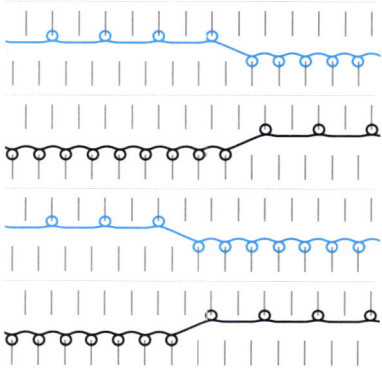

Two-color 1x1 net jacquard

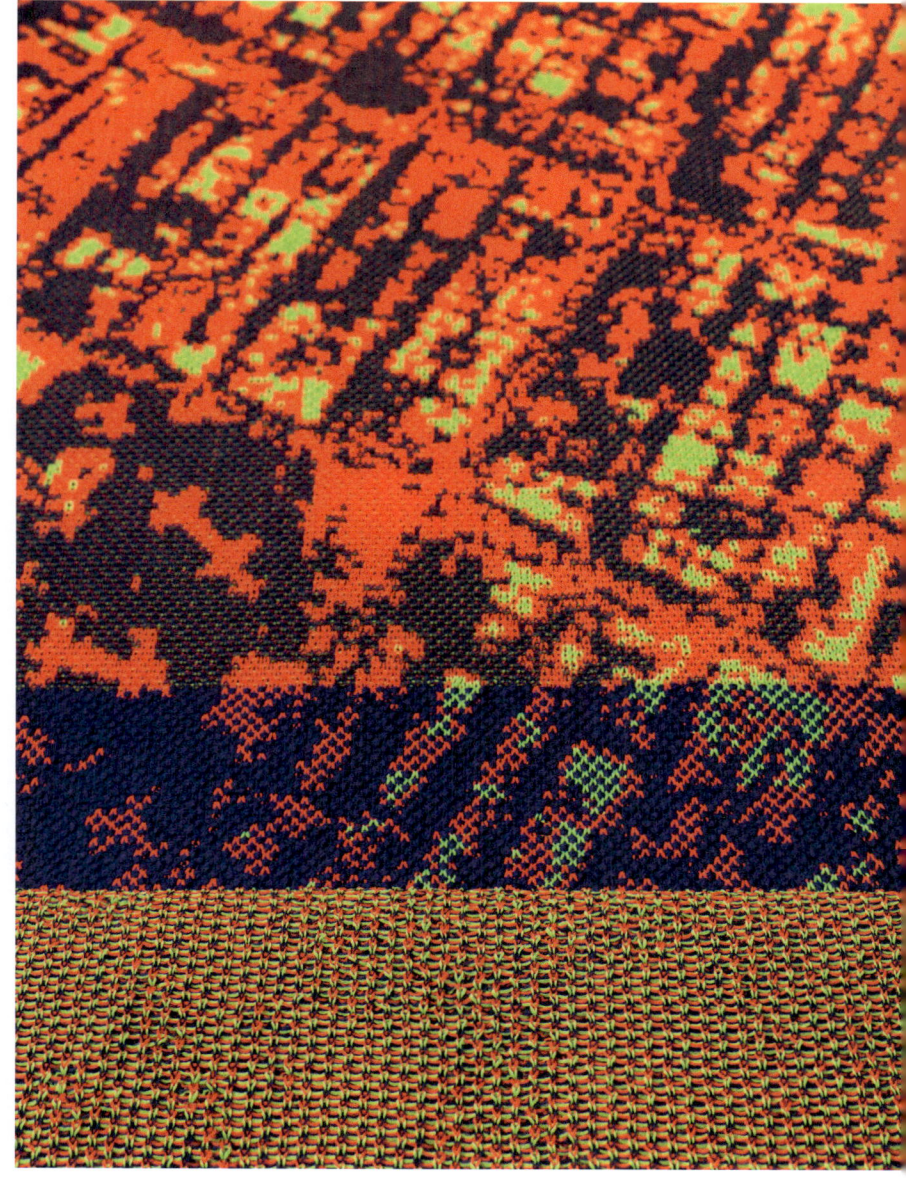

Jacquard

Relief Jacquard

Relief jacquard is also known as transfer jacquard. Depending on the jacquard type used, names will be combined, such as twill relief jacquard, etc. Relief jacquard is a double-bed jacquard. In addition to the color fields that are knitted in color on the face according to the jacquard knitting structure, it contains relief areas knitted only on the back bed in a single-jersey structure using all of the jacquard colors, resulting in them being optically mixed into a new color. The color pattern of the reverse side is characterized by the respective jacquard type. On the picture side, the reverse jersey will be visible in the relief area.

Artwork created for this type of jacquard will have an additional color designated to reliefs; for example, a two-color relief jacquard will have three-color artwork. In addition to the effect of having the colors and their mixture on the face of a fabric, the result combines different textural and structural effects as well as different levels of transparency and different draping qualities.

Fig. 1410117 shows an example of a custom three-color tubular relief jacquard whose relief areas are knitted with only one of the three yarns, and the other two float and tuck. One of the yarns is traditionally plated for an additional color effect.

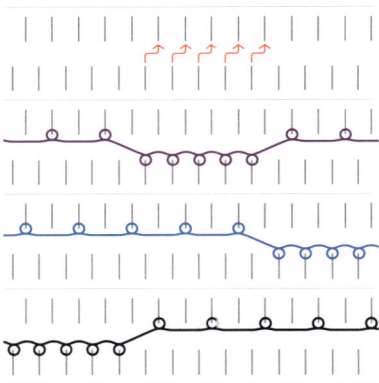

Three-color relief jacquard

1410117

NOTES

Has all the qualities of the corresponding jacquard.

ATTENTION

Pay special attention when using cross-tubular relief jacquard. When transitioning from the relief single-jersey areas to the double-bed areas, the casting-on of stitches might be necessary , depending on the artwork.

Jacquard

Plating

Technology-based color effect

Many interesting color effects can be achieved by combining different yarns together in the same stitch. The simplest way of combining different yarns together, using random or wild plating, does not rely on any specific technology or special machine parts.

Proper plating is a technology related to the yarn feeding mechanism of a machine, which carries two or more different yarns as one, while maintaining their relative position to the front and back of the stitch. Traditional plating employs a plating feeder that holds two yarns together with one visible on the front side of a knit and the other on its back.

Relatively recent technological development, such as the birth of Stoll ADF technology, which allows yarn feeders the freedom of movement independent of a carriage, expanded plating capabilities dramatically. Yarns from different feeders can be combined to form a stitch. That increases both the number of color combinations possible in one knit and the number of yarns that can be plated together (there are only two in traditional plating). For instance, if 12 yarn feeders are threaded with 12 different yarns, there are 132 (12x11) possible two-yarn color combinations. The freedom of yarn feeder movement also allows for the yarns positions to be reversed when using precise inverse plating and single-system inverse plating, as well as only plating in a selected area: selective plating.

In any plating, one yarn will be dominant on one side of the fabric, but colors of the other yarns plated with it will influence the perceived color. Complete coverage with yarns of the same or similar count (thickness) is hard to achieve; e.g., the single end of a count 15 yarn on a single count 15 will result in 50% coverage, and single count 15 on single count 30 in 90% coverage. The resulting visual effect is that of optical color mixing with little specks of covered colors shining through the dominant one (see fig. 1210024). When different colors are plated on the same base color, the color perception will be of a harmonious, overall nature. Many different painterly effects can be achieved by combining different colors and other yarn attributes through plating.

Plating

NOTES

Plating can be combined with almost any knitting structure or technology, be it simple structures like jersey, ribs, cables, and ottomans, or more sophisticated designs like plush, jacquards, and intarsias.

1210024 (front)

1210024 (back)

Plating

Random Plating

Random plating, also known as wild plating, mélange, marled, or mottled knitting, involves threading multiple yarns together in the same feeder. This results in random and uncontrollable switching between the yarns' positions in relation to the stitch front and back. In hand knitting, results are a somewhat uniform mixture of the colors used, which, depending on their values, will be perceived from a distance as a new color or as a well-distributed speckled effect. In machine knitting, unpredictable striping of the involved yarns will occur. This random and unreproducible visual effect can be a great way of creating one-of-a-kind textiles. A similar look that is predictable and reproducible can be achieved by creating artwork that can be used with inverse plating, discussed in the following chapters.

Plating

Plating

Traditional Plating

Historically, plating was mainly used for functional purposes, such as increasing the elasticity of the knit by plating with elastomeric yarn or reducing the cost by plating with inferior yarn on the back of fabric. That said, traditional plating is a great tool to introduce color into knitted fabric. Because the color and/or materiality of the front (knit) and back (purl) of the plated stitches are different, combining knit and purl stitches in the same fabric will create color patterns as well as texture. Ribs will create vertical color stripes, and basketweave will create checks. Two-color artwork translated into knit and purl knitting will have both color and texture present in a fabric. See fig. 2310006 for an example of a traditional plating combined with ribs and cables. Tuck and float stitches will alter the color as well, but in more subtle and textural ways.

Plating

Precise Inverse Plating

Machine-specific technology, such as Stoll's ADF, allows a precise switch between the yarns being plated. The resulting knit can have different colors/yarns showing on the same side of the fabric without structural change (see the stitch diagram below). Effects similar to two- or three-color jacquards can be achieved in lightweight plain single jersey without floats or backing. In fig. 1410128, a feather motif is created by switching between light and dark blue plated yarns, independent of the knit and purl structure that contributes to the dimensional effect of the feather. An additional example is fig. 1510044, where the color of the rib changes without changing its structure. Each yarn involved will be threaded into a separate yarn feeder and will need a separate knitting system to perform the switch. Precise inverse plating can be used with any imagery and number of colors within a single row of knitting, based on the number of knitting systems available and on the thicknesses of yarns that can be combined into a single stitch.

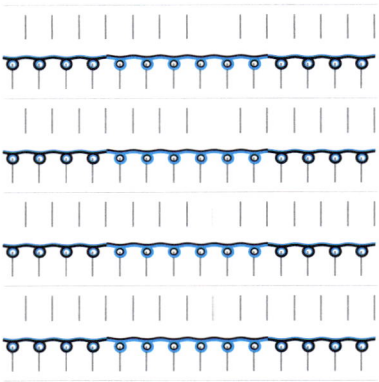

Precise inverse plating

Plating

1510044

1410128

Requires a machine with precise inverse plating capability, like Stoll ADF machines.

Artworks have to be made with care; since there is an increasing amount of color switching per row, the knitting time also increases and might become a commercial handicap.

Plating

Ikat Plating—
Single System Inverse Plating

Another inverse plating technology, such as Stoll-ikat plating®, uses a single knitting system to switch between plated yarns, which makes it a very efficient and versatile technique to manipulate color. Because only one system is involved in switching between yarns, the placement of the switch is less accurate. This results in blurred color borders in the horizontal. Colors optically flow and blend into each other, a visual effect very similar to that found in woven ikats. The sample in fig. 1510002 takes full advantage of Stoll-ikat plating®, creating a very lightweight fabric that is visually textural and rich. It is based on a four-color artwork and uses single-row striping with two yarns; each of those yarns is plated and switched between its two colors according to the artwork.

Another interesting use of Stoll-ikat plating® is to create reproducible and consistent space-dye yarn effects based on artwork, as in fig. 1610006, or to create random plating effects as discussed in 4.1, Random Plating.

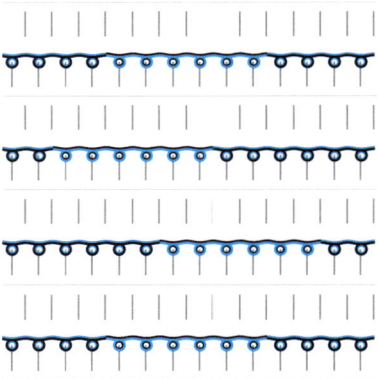

Single system inverse plating

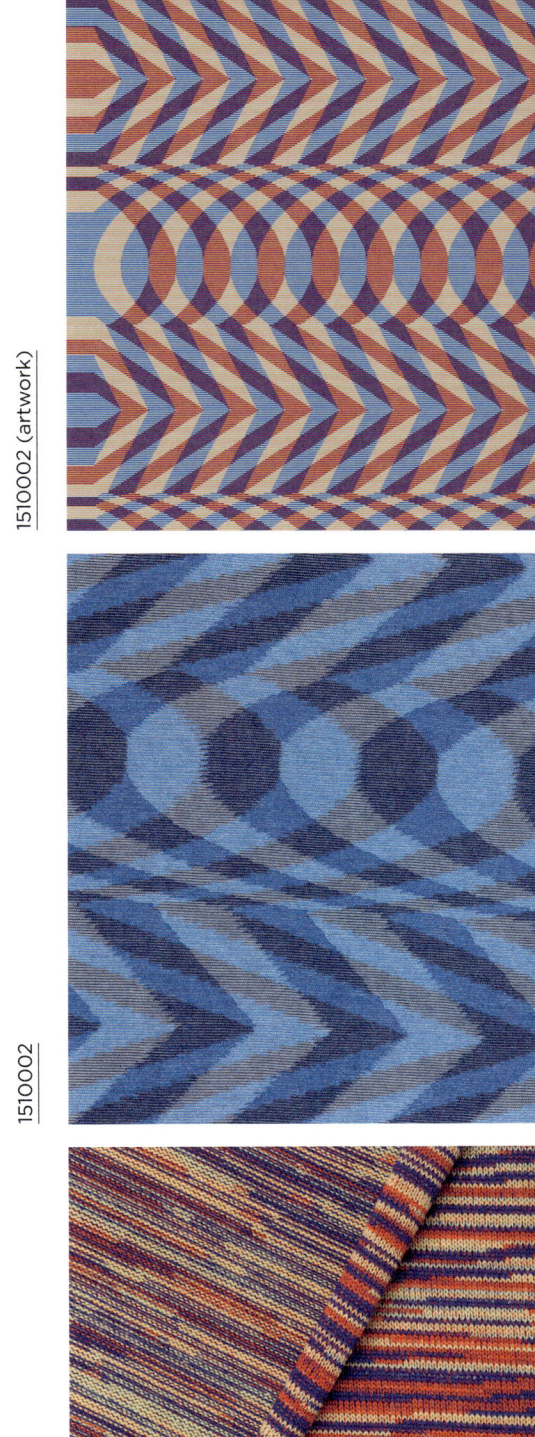

1510002 (artwork)

1510002

1610006

ATTENTION

Requires machine with single knitting system plating capability, such as Stoll-ikat plating®.

This plating method will blur crisp graphic outlines in the horizontal. See fig. 1510002 above, which shows an image and the resulting fabric.

Artwork suitable for this method will require areas of at least two inches of the same color; smaller areas of color change might not show up. That said, there are workaround solutions for double-bed knitted structures, which will allow for finer artwork details.

Plating

Selective Plating

Selective plating relies on machine-specific plating technology, like Stoll's ADF. This technology's advantage: the freedom of the yarn feeders' movement allows for plating in a selected part of a knitted row only (see stitch diagram below). The base yarn is knitted throughout the full row, while the plated yarn can join within a specific area, similar to intarsia. Selective plating can be combined with any of the inverse plating approaches described above. Fig. 1910047 shows the different color yarns selectively plated over the beige base yarn that runs throughout a knit. An even more complicated example that uses both selective and inverse plating is shown in fig. 1410097.

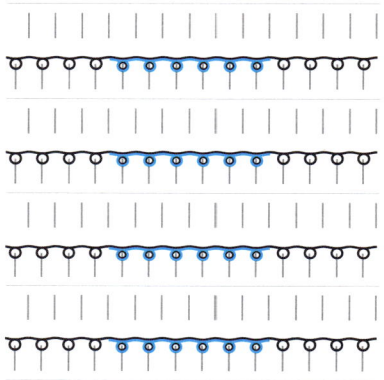

Selective plating

1910047

ATTENTION

Requires machine with selective plating capability, such as Stoll ADF machines.

1410097

Plating

Elongated Stitch

Color effect that can be achieved with either technology or structure

Elongated stitch, also known as drive lace or mesh knitting, is an effect that creates large, in comparison to machine gauge, stitches. It can be done in full rows, in single stitches, or in groups. There are two different ways to elongate a stitch. The first one is a structural approach where a new stitch is picked up on the empty needle opposite of the stitch that needs to be elongated, and sequentially dropped or cast off. The extra yarn of that stitch will go into the target stitch and elongate it (fig. 0810433). Another way is to use technology that individually controls the stitch length of any single stitch within the knitting, such as Stoll-Power Tension Setting (PTS) technology.

Resulting color effects include translucency within the areas of elongated stitches and changes in color value, where areas of looser stitches will appear lighter in color (see fig. 1410172). In addition, different graphic effects and optical illusion can be obtained when elongated stitches are combined with single row striping, including optical color mixing. Fig. 1410172 shows an example similar to that in fig. 1510002 (see a detailed description in chapter 4.4, Single System Inverse Plating). However, in addition to plating and striping, elongated stitches are introduced to extend the original four colors of fig. 1510002 sample into an eight-color scheme without any new yarns involved, just by creating new optical color mixtures (more details in 5.2, Cast-off Elongated Stitch).

Elongated Stitch

0810433

1410172

1510002

Elongated Stitch

PTS Elongated Stitch

Elongated stitches are created not by altering the structure of the knit, but by controlling the length of the chosen stitches. This level of precise control is provided by technology such as PTS. Different stitch lengths can be set during the programing process. Fig. 1410162 on the right shows the graphic artwork with diamond shapes of the PTS elongated stitches and the resulting fabric below. The additional marled or mottled color effect in this example is achieved with Stoll-ikat plating® and can be seen in the artwork as well.

Elongated Stitch

1410162 (artwork)

1410162

Elongated Stitch

Cast-off Elongated Stitch

An elongated stitch is created by picking up a stitch on an empty needle on the opposite bed and casting it off immediately or after a few rows of knitting (see the stitch diagram). The extra yarn that created this dropped stitch will travel into the stitch on a bed opposite and elongate it. The resulting knit will have transparency as well as volume in the elongated areas. When combined with single-row striping of different colors, as seen in fig. 1010443, the yarn color of the elongated stitch becomes more dominant and changes the color proportions within the optical color mixture of its area. In fig. 1010443, two different optical color mixtures are created: elongated stitches in the lighter (beige) yarn and elongated stitches in the darker (black) yarn, while white yarn is introduced only in certain areas with intarsia. Fig. 0710429 presents an additional example of imagery created with two-color striping and elongated stitches within a 3x3 rib structure.

In addition, this structure can be used with thicker yarns to create fabrics that are bulkier than the machine gauge, as well as successfully combine yarns of different thicknesses (counts) in the same knit.

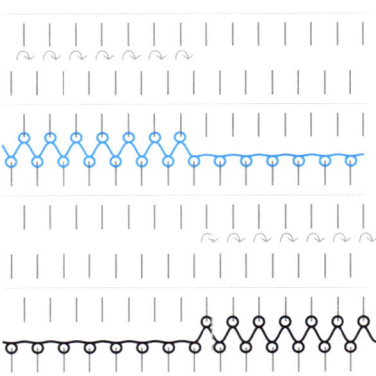

Cast-off elongated stitch

Elongated Stitch

NOTES

Cast-off elongation can be done on any machine.

PTS elongation can be combined with any other structure; cast-off elongation can be combined with any structure as well, as long as needle occupancy allows it.

Elongated stitches, PTS or cast-off, can be used to compensate for different lengths between various knitting structures.

PTS can be used to loosen edge stitches for better results during decreases in fully fashioned shaping.

Elongated stitches combined with single-row striping of different color yarns can be used to create light single-jersey fabric with graphics not suitable for float jacquard.

ATTENTION

Areas of elongated stitches create volume and distortion within a fabric. If elongation occurs repeatedly in the same place within the rows, the fabric will have volume in those areas and will not be flat. This could be used intentionally to create shape and/or to create draping.

1010443

0710429

Elongated Stitch

Plush

Structure-based color effect supported by technology and specific machine setup

Plush, also known as pile, knitted terry, and fur knit, is a single-jersey knitting technique that involves two yarns knitted together: binding or base yarn (blue in the diagram below) and plush yarn (black). The binding yarn always forms a stitch. The plush yarn forms a stitch together with the binding yarn while plated behind it, and can create a loop extending outward (pile) at the purl side of the fabric. The pile loop is created by picking up stitches, with plush yarn only, on the empty needles of the opposing bed and casting them off. Pile can be created on either side of the fabric by alternating the needle arrangement between the beds, but not on both sides simultaneously. The resulting fabric is in relief and highly dimensional with combined raised (plush) and impressed (base) areas. Multiple plush yarns can be used together to create fuller, opulent pile or to alternate yarns of the plush with inverse plating techniques, such as Stoll-ikat plating®, or to change the color or texture within plush areas, as shown in fig. 2110050 and in fig. 1810119, of both binding and plush yarns.

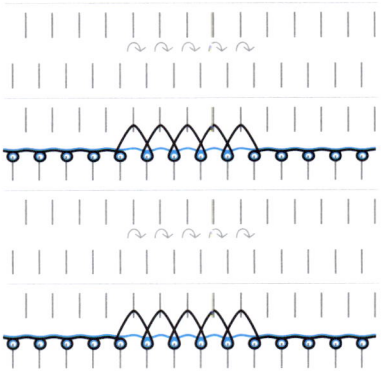

Plush

1810119

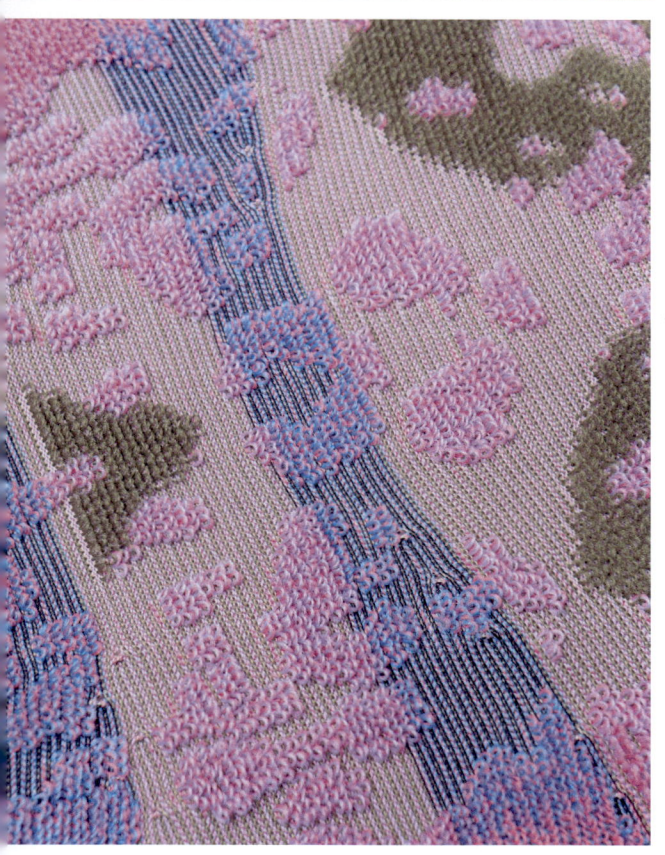

2110050

Combinable with other ADF techniques such as Stoll-ikat plating® and Stoll-weave-in®, shown in fig. 1810119.

Can be applied to a full row of knitting as well as to a selected area, as in intarsia or partial knitting.

ATTENTION

Requires a Stoll plush device and a specific machine setup.

Plush

Devoré

Technology-based color effect supported by specific machine setup

Devoré, also known as burnout, filigree, fishnet, mesh stitch, or thread-lace jacquard, is a single-jersey knitting technique that involves two yarns knitted together: a binding yarn (black in the diagram below) and a main or motif yarn (blue). The binding yarn always forms a stitch. The motif yarn can either form a stitch together with the binding yarn and be plated behind it, or float behind the binding yarn stitch. This structure can be thought of as a hybrid of plating and float jacquard. Devoré can be applied to a full row of knitting as well as to a selected area (combined with intarsia or partial knitting). In addition, the roles of main and binding yarns can be switched at any point throughout the knit.

When very fine or transparent yarn is used as a binding yarn, the visual effect will be lace-like or appear as if the knitting is unraveling, resembling that of a classic devoré printing technique that combines areas of transparency and opacity (see fig. 1210144). This technique creates areas of different thicknesses, which will affect fabric performance qualities, such as stretch and breathability.

Additional subtle color effects can be achieved by using two yarns of the same or similar colors (fig. 2110005) or by reversing the fabric and using the floats as a visual element (fig. 2110045).

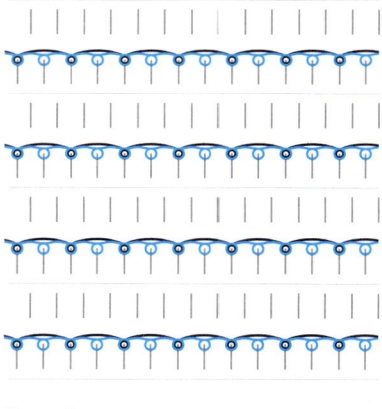

Devoré

Devoré

1210144

2110005

NOTES

Long floats can be created and clipped if one of the yarns used is elastomeric.

ATTENTION

Requires a Stoll-devoré® kit and a specific machine setup.

2110045

Devoré

Weave-in
Structure-based color effect

Knit-weaving, also known as inlay, weft insertion, or weave-in, is a family of different knitted structures that allow for the secondary yarn to be inserted horizontally into the knit in a weave-like manner. In most weave-in structures, the secondary yarn will never form a stitch by going into the needle hook. Rather, it will travel from the front to the back of the fabric between the stitches, similar to a running stitch; the secondary yarn can be attached to the surface of the fabric by additional knitting yarn like a couching stitch, or it can float between the knitted layers as filler yarn. Knit-weaving is essentially a yarn floating within a knitting structure, and there are no visible differences between the knit-weaving and float. The former has the advantage of allowing for very long float sections due to a machine part, such as Stoll's weave-in device. The weave-in device holds the float in place for safe knitting formation. It also permits the safe incorporation of materials into the knit that are otherwise not suitable for knitting, such as materials that cannot form a stitch because they are too thick (in relation to machine gauge), too hard, too stiff, or too brittle. The presence of the float will limit the inherent stretch of the knit in the horizontal but will not affect the vertical stretch. That said, the inlayed material/yarn should have some stretch to it to prevent it from buckling out of the fabric, because the knitted fabric shrinks.

All the weave-in structures mentioned above can be applied to a full row of knitting as well as to a selected area (intarsia or partial knitting), as shown in fig. 1810036. If the inlay yarn is suitable for knitting and can form a stitch, the roles between the main and inlay yarns can be switched throughout the knit, as seen in fig. 1510042.

Resulting color effects include optical color mixing, layering, transparency, and fine horizontal lines, as well as the mimicking of warp and weft structures characteristic of weaving. The color saturation of the weaved-in yarn can be increased by weaving-in twice (or more). Doing so will increase the fabric weight as well and can be used to completely mask the color of the background yarn.

1810036

NOTES

There is no biasing (torquing) when single-ply yarn is used as a weave-in, as opposed to use in single jersey.

Knit-weaving can be done on any machine; on Stoll machines, it is supported by the Stoll-weave-in® technique and use of a machine part called a weave-in device.

ATTENTION

Weave-in might be problematic with a tightly knitted base or when partially knitting.

To prevent snagging when multiple yarn ends are laid-in together, twine them together before knitting.

1510042

Weave-in

Technology 173

Running Stitch Weave-in

This technique is based on structures having both knit and purl stitches or stitch transferring, as in pointelle. The needle arrangement, which has some stitches on both beds, creates a path in which inlay yarn can be placed. The needle arrangement can be constant (e.g., 1x1, 2x2, or any other rib); interchangeable, such as moss and rice stitches; or temporary, such as pointelle or any other transfer of the stitch back and forth between the beds (shown in fig. 1910027).

The resulting fabric visually resembles woven textile with the inlay yarn forming the weft, and the knitting yarn the warp (see fig. 2110029). In fig. 1910027 an additional color in the background is introduced with Stoll-ikat plating®.

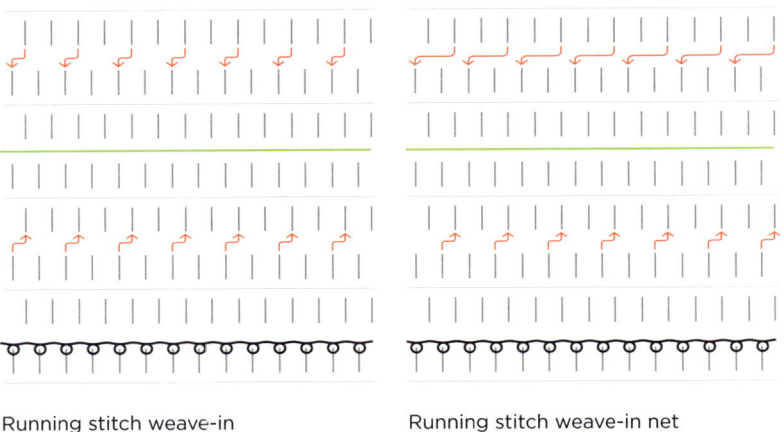

Running stitch weave-in

Running stitch weave-in net

1910027

2110029

Couching Stitch Weave-in

Inlay yarn (the green yarn in the stitch notation), is usually attached to the purl side of the knit by couching yarn (orange in the same diagram) similar or different from the main knitting yarn (black). In the area of the knit where the couching stitch weave-in is formed, the main yarn is knitted on a single bed, while the couching yarn is tucked between the knit and empty needles of the opposite bed. This creates a channel in which to place the inlay. Once placed, the inlay is secured by transferring the couching yarn's tucks of empty needles back to the main knit and attaching the inlay to it (fig. 1910024 and fig. 1910063). The material choices for the three yarns used (inlay, couching, base), as well as the density and patterning of the couching tucks, will achieve different color effects.

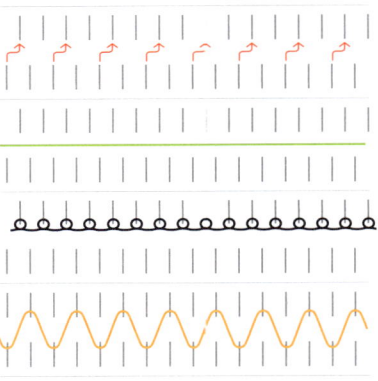

Couching stitch weave-in

1910063

1910024 (front)

Weave-in

Filler Weave-in

This technique is based on on a tubular or cross-tubular structure. Two or more layers of fabric are knitted with the main or knitting yarn(s), while secondary or inlay yarn floats between them, secured at the edges and/or anytime the main yarn crosses from one bed to another (see fig. 2010001). Depending on the inlay and main yarn's materiality, this structure will result in an embossed, quilted-like puffy volume, or layered and overlapping effects with wiggly horizontal lines of the filler yarn showing through the transparent front layer.

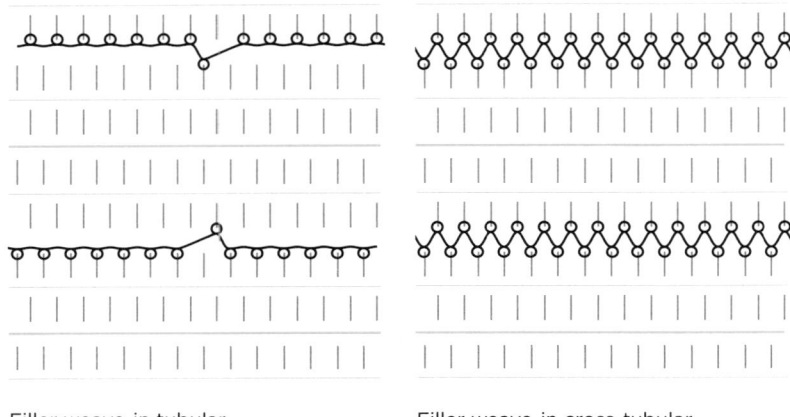

Filler weave-in tubular

Filler weave-in cross-tubular

Weave-in

Weave-in

Matrix

		Page 17 **1710036**	Page 14 **1510059**	Page 13 **1810116**	Page 12 **1510063**
Stripes	1.0	◯			◯
Intarsia	2.0				◯
Float Jacquard	3.1				
Twill Jacquard	3.2				
Stripe Jacquard	3.3				
Cross-Tubular Jacquard	3.4				
Net Jacquard	3.5				
Relief Jacquard	3.6	◯			
Random Plating	4.1				
Traditional Plating	4.2			◯	
Precise Inverse Plating	4.3				
Stoll-ikat plating®	4.4	◯	◯		
Selective Plating	4.5				
PTS Elongated Stitch	5.1				
Cast-off Elongated Stitch	5.2				◯
Plush	6.0				
Devoré	7.0				
Stoll-weave-in®	8.0		◯	◯	

Page 11	Page 15	Page 10	Page 20	Page 21	Page 22
2110064	**2110062**	**2310001**	**2210023**	**2110065**	**1210036**

		Page 27 **1110385**	Page 18 **1510042**	Page 26 **0810458**	Page 24 **1210041**
Stripes	1.0			○	
Intarsia	2.0	○		○	○
Float Jacquard	3.1				
Twill Jacquard	3.2				
Stripe Jacquard	3.3				
Cross-Tubular Jacquard	3.4		○	○	
Net Jacquard	3.5				
Relief Jacquard	3.6				
Random Plating	4.1				
Traditional Plating	4.2				
Precise Inverse Plating	4.3		○		
Stoll-ikat plating®	4.4		○		
Selective Plating	4.5				
PTS Elongated Stitch	5.1				
Cast-off Elongated Stitch	5.2				
Plush	6.0				
Devoré	7.0				
Stoll-weave-in®	8.0		○		

Page 23
1210181

Page 25
2210019

Page 28
1410162

Page 29
1410160

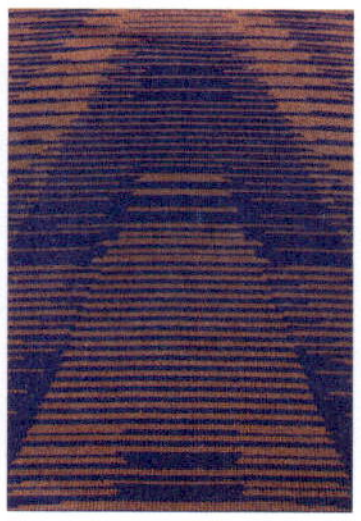

Page 30
1210227

Page 31
2310002

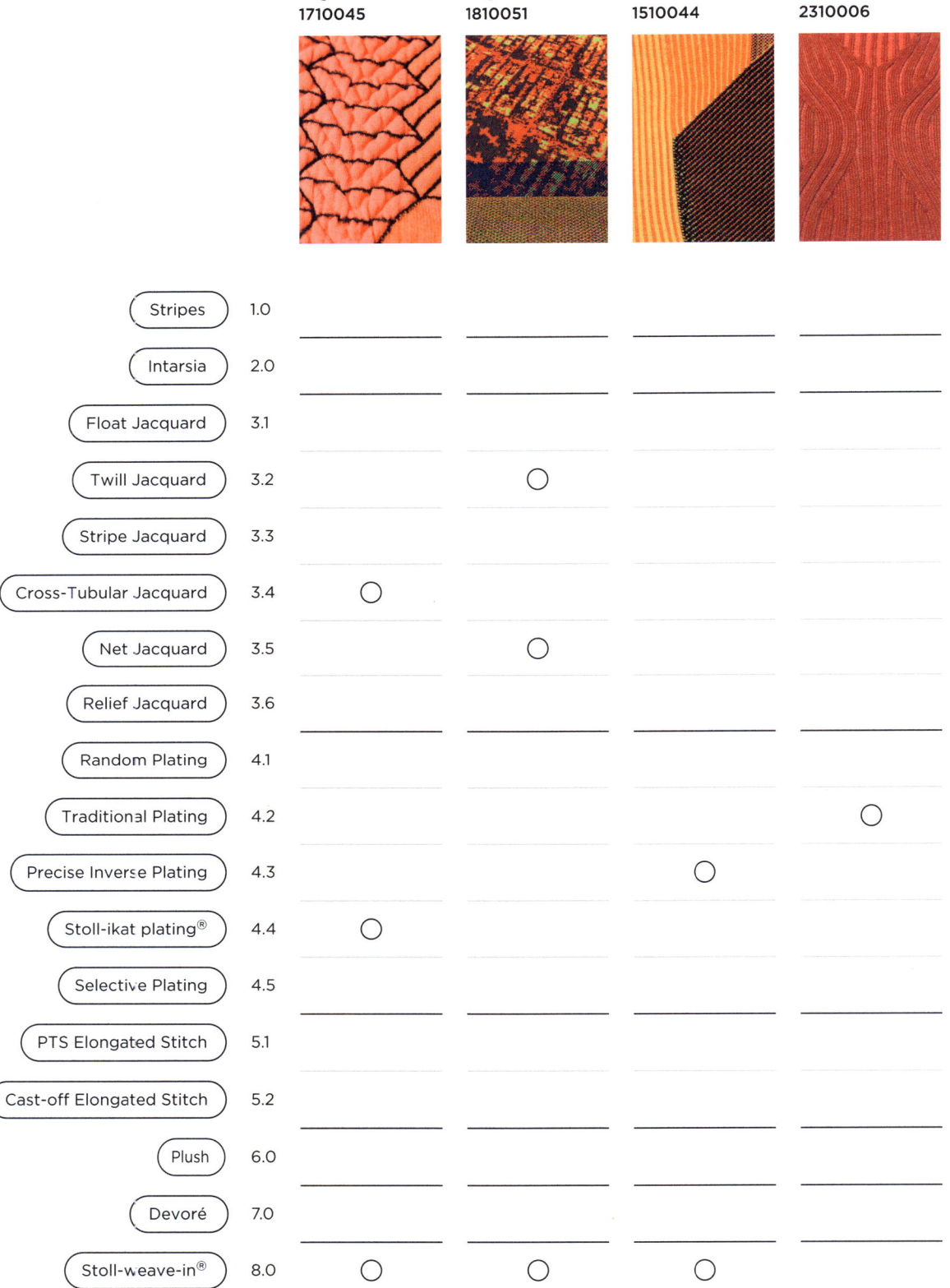

		Page 35 **1710045**	Page 33 **1810051**	Page 34 **1510044**	Page 37 **2310006**
Stripes	1.0				
Intarsia	2.0				
Float Jacquard	3.1				
Twill Jacquard	3.2		○		
Stripe Jacquard	3.3				
Cross-Tubular Jacquard	3.4	○			
Net Jacquard	3.5		○		
Relief Jacquard	3.6				
Random Plating	4.1				
Traditional Plating	4.2				○
Precise Inverse Plating	4.3			○	
Stoll-ikat plating®	4.4	○			
Selective Plating	4.5				
PTS Elongated Stitch	5.1				
Cast-off Elongated Stitch	5.2				
Plush	6.0				
Devoré	7.0				
Stoll-weave-in®	8.0	○	○	○	

Page 38
1210059

Page 40
1510102

Page 36
1210144

Page 39
1210157

Page 41
2210029

Page 42
2210034

		Page 43 **0610281**	Page 44 **1210024**	Page 45 **1610006**	Page 46 **0610427**
Stripes	1.0	○	○		
Intarsia	2.0	○			○
Float Jacquard	3.1				
Twill Jacquard	3.2				○
Stripe Jacquard	3.3				
Cross-Tubular Jacquard	3.4				○
Net Jacquard	3.5				
Relief Jacquard	3.6				
Random Plating	4.1				
Traditional Plating	4.2				
Precise Inverse Plating	4.3		○		
Stoll-ikat plating®	4.4			○	
Selective Plating	4.5				
PTS Elongated Stitch	5.1				
Cast-off Elongated Stitch	5.2				○
Plush	6.0				
Devoré	7.0				
Stoll-weave-in®	8.0				

Page 47
1910078

Page 50
2110045

Page 49
2110005

Page 48
1910052

Page 51
2210039

Page 52
1810097

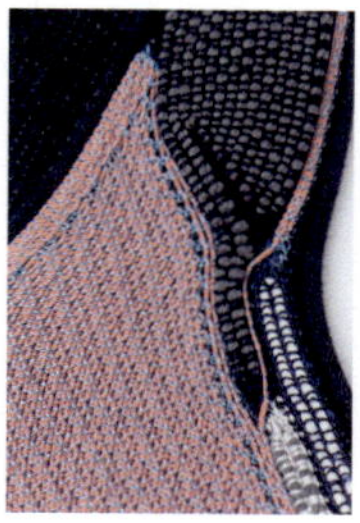

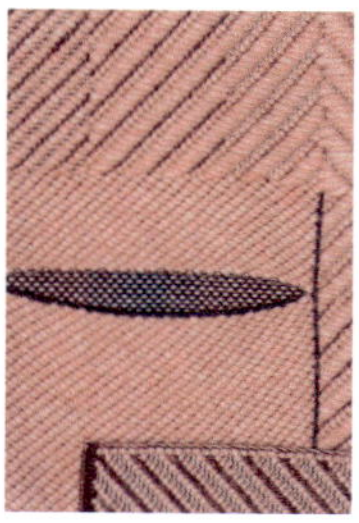

		Page 53 **2110058**	Page 55 **1810118**	Page 54 **1610056**	Page 56 **2210027**
Stripes	1.0	○			
Intarsia	2.0	○			
Float Jacquard	3.1		○		
Twill Jacquard	3.2				
Stripe Jacquard	3.3				
Cross-Tubular Jacquard	3.4	○		○	
Net Jacquard	3.5				
Relief Jacquard	3.6				
Random Plating	4.1				
Traditional Plating	4.2				○
Precise Inverse Plating	4.3	○			
Stoll-ikat plating®	4.4	○		○	
Selective Plating	4.5		○		
PTS Elongated Stitch	5.1				
Cast-off Elongated Stitch	5.2				
Plush	6.0				
Devoré	7.0				
Stoll-weave-in®	8.0				

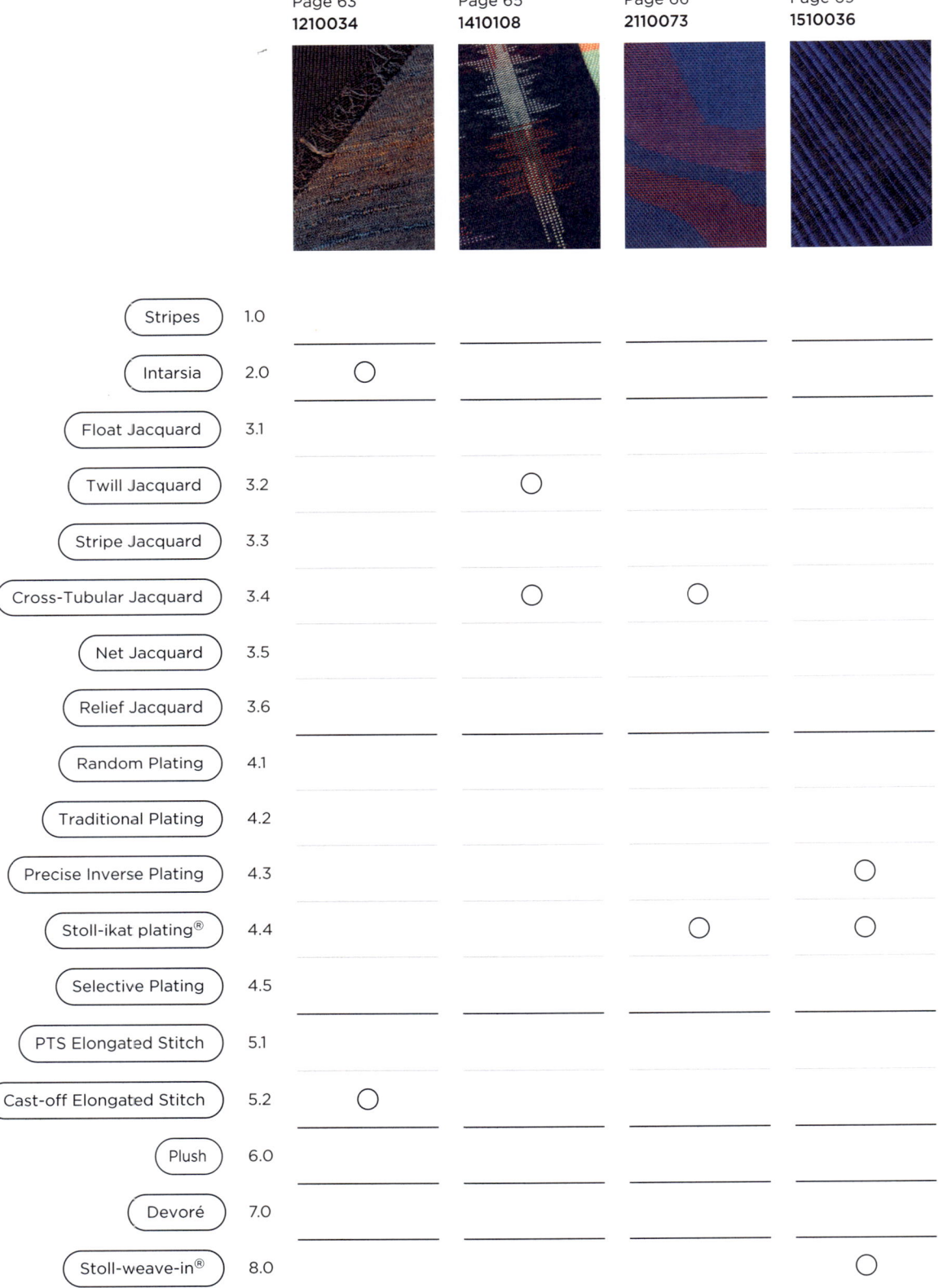

		Page 63 **1210034**	Page 65 **1410108**	Page 66 **2110073**	Page 69 **1510036**
Stripes	1.0				
Intarsia	2.0	○			
Float Jacquard	3.1				
Twill Jacquard	3.2		○		
Stripe Jacquard	3.3				
Cross-Tubular Jacquard	3.4		○	○	
Net Jacquard	3.5				
Relief Jacquard	3.6				
Random Plating	4.1				
Traditional Plating	4.2				
Precise Inverse Plating	4.3				○
Stoll-ikat plating®	4.4			○	○
Selective Plating	4.5				
PTS Elongated Stitch	5.1				
Cast-off Elongated Stitch	5.2	○			
Plush	6.0				
Devoré	7.0				
Stoll-weave-in®	8.0				○

Page 68 **1710022** 	Page 70 **2310004** 	Page 72 **1410128** 	Page 73 **1410097** 	Page 71 **1510055** 	Page 74 **1610003** 
○				○	
					○
					○
		○	○		
					○
○			○		
					○
	○				

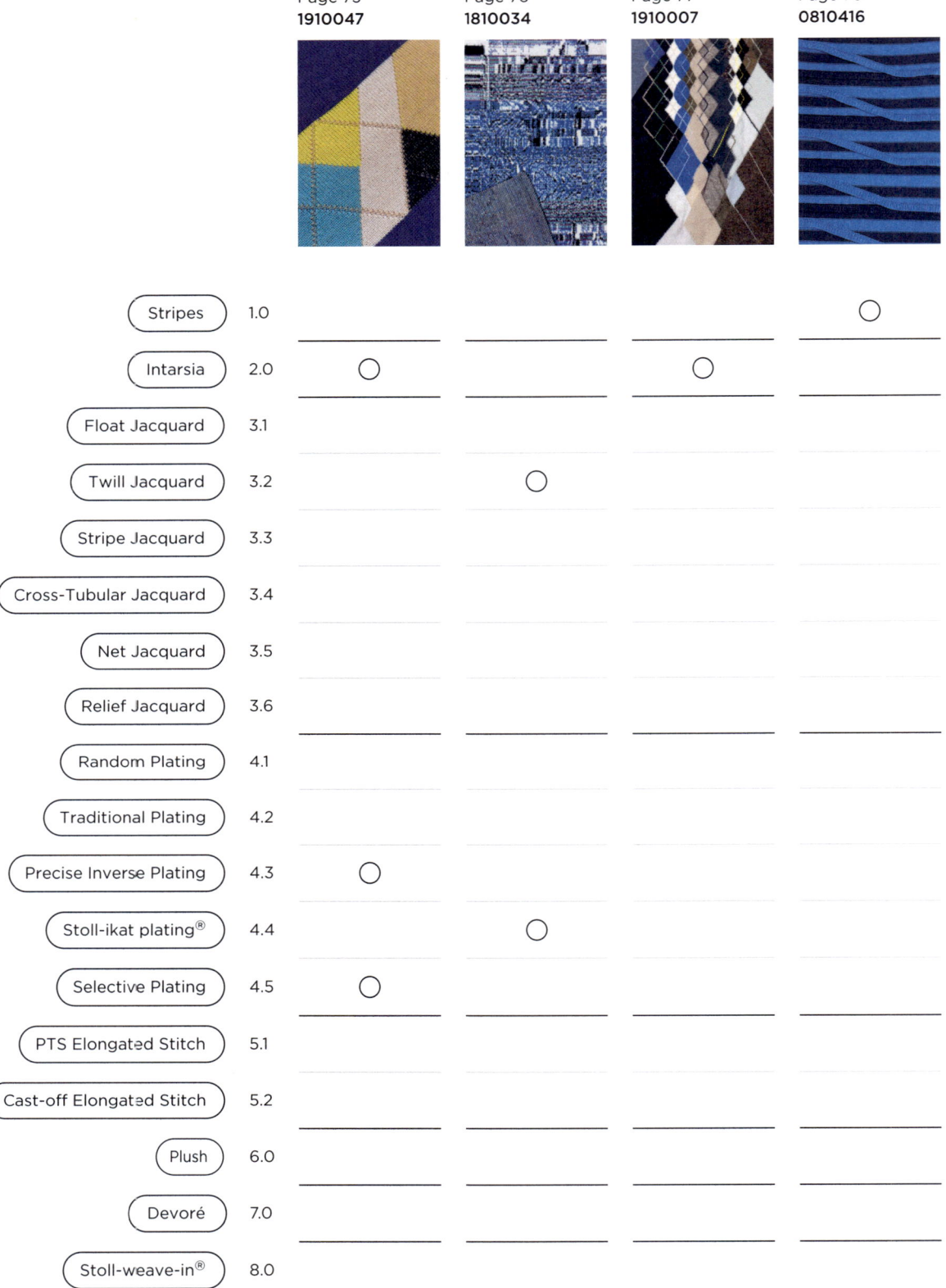

		Page 75 **1910047**	Page 76 **1810034**	Page 77 **1910007**	Page 78 **0810416**
Stripes	1.0				○
Intarsia	2.0	○		○	
Float Jacquard	3.1				
Twill Jacquard	3.2		○		
Stripe Jacquard	3.3				
Cross-Tubular Jacquard	3.4				
Net Jacquard	3.5				
Relief Jacquard	3.6				
Random Plating	4.1				
Traditional Plating	4.2				
Precise Inverse Plating	4.3	○			
Stoll-ikat plating®	4.4		○		
Selective Plating	4.5	○			
PTS Elongated Stitch	5.1				
Cast-off Elongated Stitch	5.2				
Plush	6.0				
Devoré	7.0				
Stoll-weave-in®	8.0				

Page 79 **0810433** 	Page 82 **1410161** 	Page 83 **1410172** 	Page 81 **0810408** 	Page 80 **0810454** 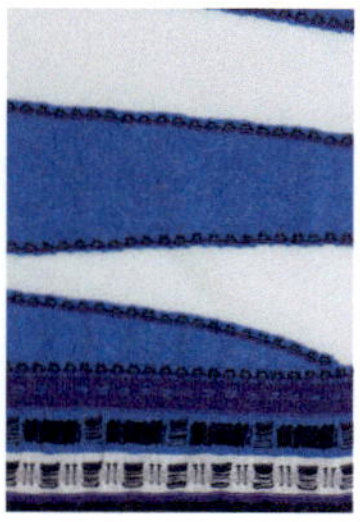	Page 85 **1210177** 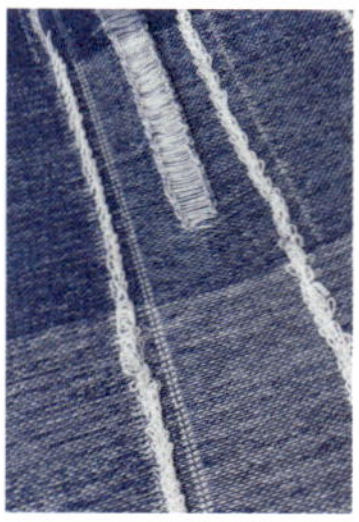

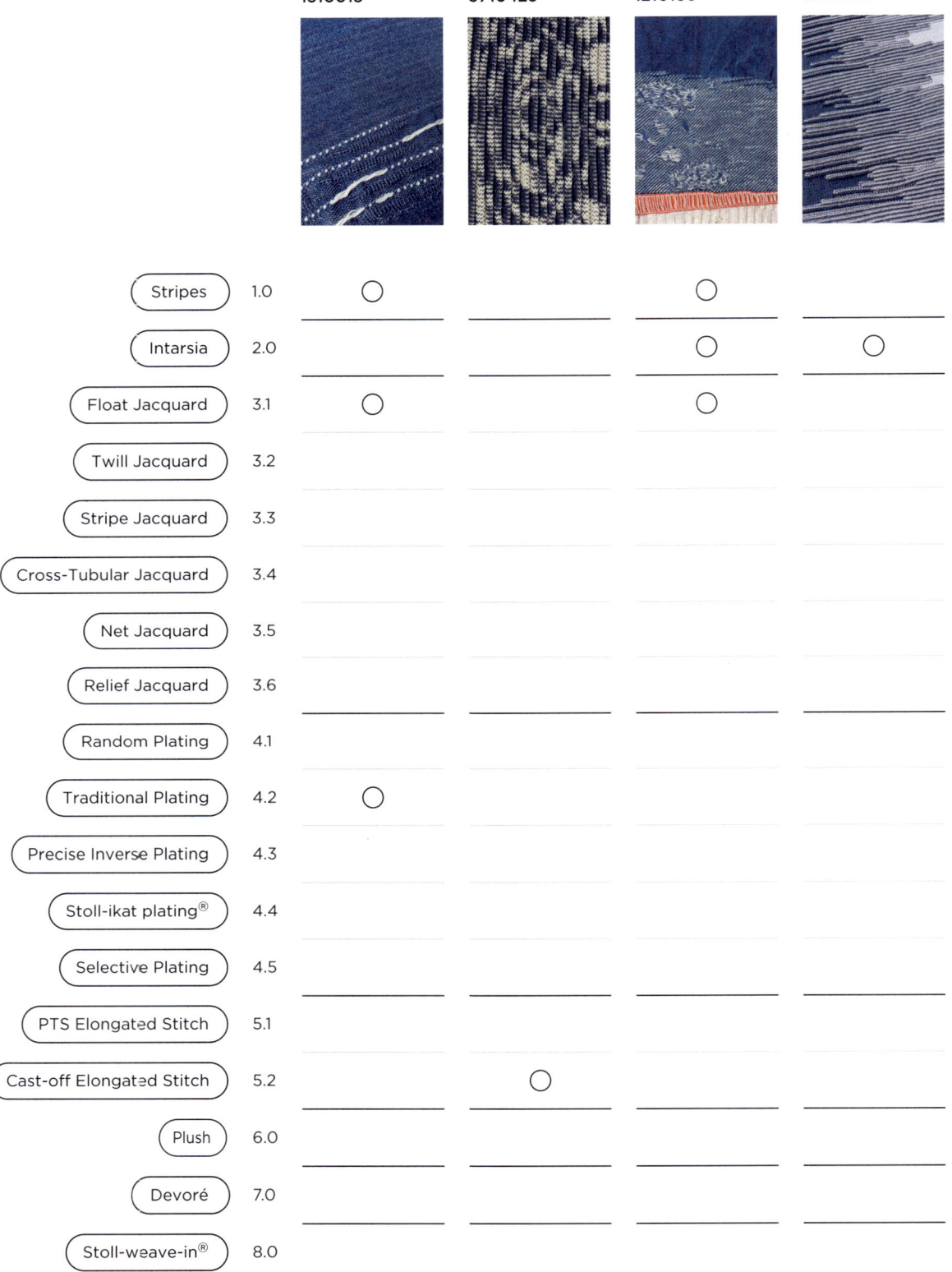

		Page 86 **1310018**	Page 87 **0710429**	Page 84 **1210166**	Page 87 **0510021**
Stripes	1.0	○		○	
Intarsia	2.0			○	○
Float Jacquard	3.1	○		○	
Twill Jacquard	3.2				
Stripe Jacquard	3.3				
Cross-Tubular Jacquard	3.4				
Net Jacquard	3.5				
Relief Jacquard	3.6				
Random Plating	4.1				
Traditional Plating	4.2	○			
Precise Inverse Plating	4.3				
Stoll-ikat plating®	4.4				
Selective Plating	4.5				
PTS Elongated Stitch	5.1				
Cast-off Elongated Stitch	5.2		○		
Plush	6.0				
Devoré	7.0				
Stoll-weave-in®	8.0				

Page 88	Page 89	Page 93	Page 91	Page 90	Page 92
0910622	**1310079**	**1510002**	**2010001**	**1910063**	**1610053**

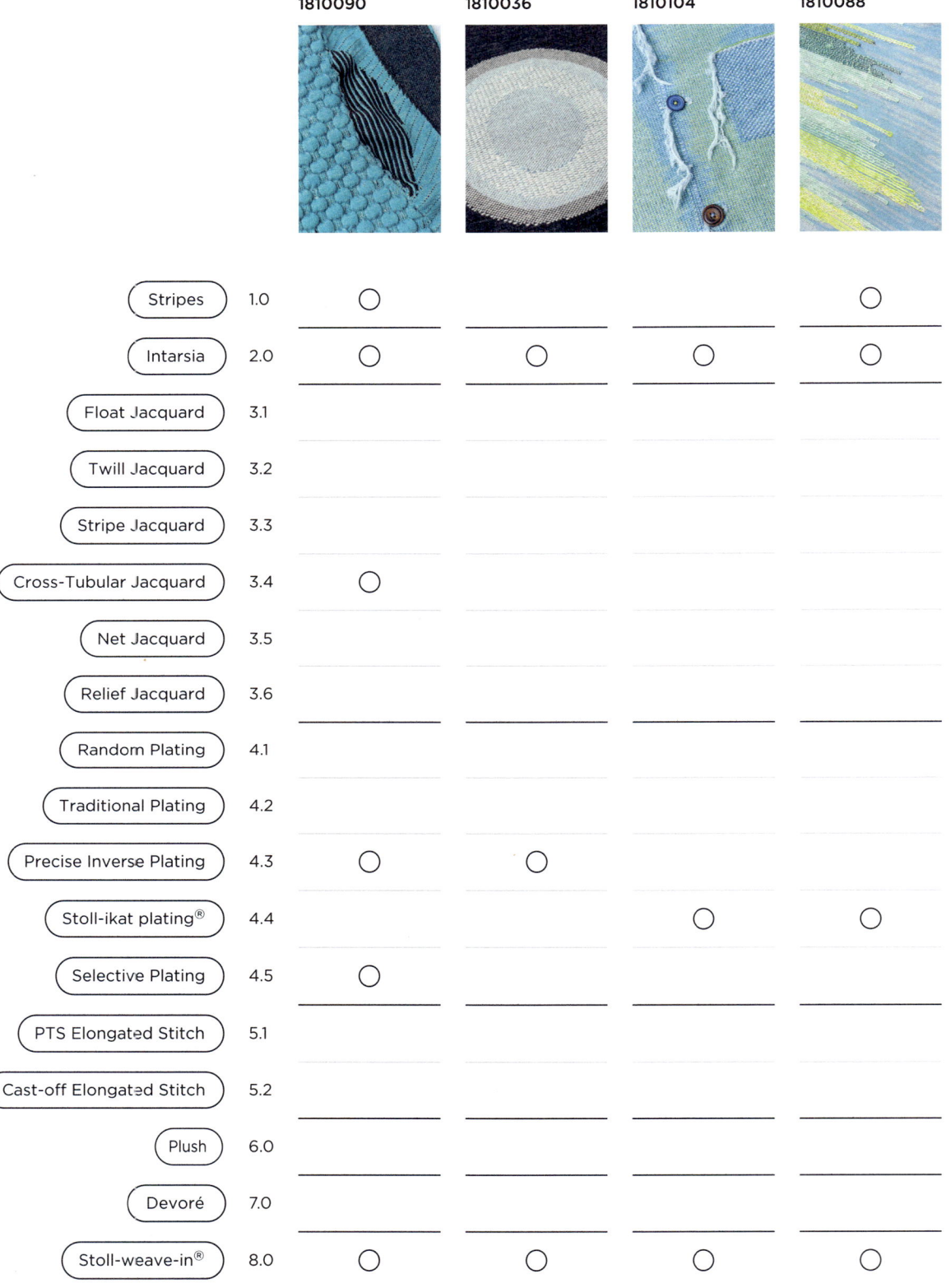

		Page 95 **1810090**	Page 97 **1810036**	Page 94 **1810104**	Page 96 **1810088**
Stripes	1.0	○			○
Intarsia	2.0	○	○	○	○
Float Jacquard	3.1				
Twill Jacquard	3.2				
Stripe Jacquard	3.3				
Cross-Tubular Jacquard	3.4	○			
Net Jacquard	3.5				
Relief Jacquard	3.6				
Random Plating	4.1				
Traditional Plating	4.2				
Precise Inverse Plating	4.3	○	○		
Stoll-ikat plating®	4.4			○	○
Selective Plating	4.5	○			
PTS Elongated Stitch	5.1				
Cast-off Elongated Stitch	5.2				
Plush	6.0				
Devoré	7.0				
Stoll-weave-in®	8.0	○	○	○	○

Page 101
2210026

Page 100
1910024

Page 99
1810119

Page 102
1810124

Page 103
1910027

Page 105
1810063

		Page 106 **1910042**	Page 104 **2110029**	Page 107 **1010443**	Page 108 **2110072**
Stripes	1.0		○	○	○
Intarsia	2.0	○			
Float Jacquard	3.1				
Twill Jacquard	3.2				
Stripe Jacquard	3.3				
Cross-Tubular Jacquard	3.4				
Net Jacquard	3.5				
Relief Jacquard	3.6				
Random Plating	4.1				
Traditional Plating	4.2				
Precise Inverse Plating	4.3				
Stoll-ikat plating®	4.4		○		○
Selective Plating	4.5	○			
PTS Elongated Stitch	5.1				
Cast-off Elongated Stitch	5.2			○	
Plush	6.0				○
Devoré	7.0	○			
Stoll-weave-in®	8.0		○		

Glossary

ADF, or Autarc Direct Feeding: a new generation of Stoll knitting machines that define an entirely new standard and open up unrivalled knitting dimensions due to its innovative yarn carrier technology. Autarc Direct Feeding describes the yarn carriers' ability to move freely and independently of the carriage, both horizontally and vertically.

Burnout: same as **devoré.**

Carriage, in knitting: a manually or motorized moving part of a knitting machine that slides across the needle beds. A carriage carries the yarn feeders, raises selected needles into various working positions to form a stitch, as in knit, tuck, float, etc., and performs needle actions, such as transfer, cast-off, etc.

Color field: in this text, area of color in an artwork or a knit bordered on the right and left by an area of a different color or by the knit's vertical edges; defined for each knitting row.

Color jacquards, in knitting: a family of multicolor pattern knitting structures.

Color value: the lightness or darkness of a color.

Couching stitch, in embroidery: couching and laid work are techniques in which yarn or other materials are laid across the surface of the ground fabric and fastened in place with small stitches of the same or different yarn.

Cut and sew, in knitting: a production method based on cutting sewing patterns out of rectangular panels knitted to size or from knitted yardage. Cut pieces are sewn together into the final product.

Devoré: a burnout technique for velvet fabrics, where mixed-fiber material undergoes a chemical process to dissolve cellulose fibers to create a semi-transparent pattern against a more solidly woven fabric. Devoré can also refer to a velvet fabric with a pattern formed by burning the pile away with acid.

Face: the side of the fabric that is chosen as its front side.

Filigree: ornamental work of fine wire (typically gold or silver) formed into delicate tracery.

Fully fashioned, in knitting: a production method based on knitting shaped panels by decreasing and increasing the number of stitches in a row. Increases and decreases are usually placed a few stitches in from the panel edge and create a visible mark called a fully fashioned mark. Shaped pieces are linked together into the final product.

Inlay: a decorative technique used to create an ornamental design, pattern, or scene by inserting or setting into a shallow or depressed ground or surface a material of a different color or type.

Integral knitting: a production method based on tubular knitting, such as **Stoll-knit and wear®,** in which an entire product or the majority of it is knitted as a whole and does not require cutting or sewing.

Ikat: a textile woven with weft and/or warp yarns that are resist-dyed prior to weaving to create a color pattern in the final cloth. This method lends a blurriness, characteristic of ikat, to the pattern in the horizontal and/or vertical.

Jacquard, in weaving: a warp selection apparatus, originally operated with perforated cards, fitted to a loom to facilitate the weaving of figured and brocaded fabrics. Also refers to a fabric, woven on a jacquard loom, of an intricate variegated weave or pattern.

Jacquard, in knitting: historically refers to any knitting structure that employs needle selection. The most common use of the term jacquard in knitting, short for color jacquard: needle selective, multicolor pattern knitting structures.

Knit: in this text, refers to both front stitch and knitted fabric.

Knitting or stitch structure, in knitting: the manner in which yarns intermesh in knitted fabrics.

Knitting technique, in knitting: a way of knitting independent of knitting structure, such as partial knitting or plating, defined by a machine's technical abilities and/or carriage movement.

Machine gauge, in knitting: the number of needles within one inch of the needle bed. The larger the number (more needles placed together within an inch) the finer the gauge and the resulting fabric, and the finer the yarn to be used.

Optical color mixing: the perception of color resulting from the combination of adjacent colors.

Partial knitting, in knitting: same as **short rowing** and **gores.** This technique knits only part of a row. The principle is similar to intarsia.

Plating, in knitting: two (or more) different yarns are held consistently in the same relative position to the front and back of the knitted loop/stitch.

Plating feeder, in knitting: in traditional plating, a yarn feeder carries two yarns, main and secondary, and maintains the constant relationship between the yarns while forming a stitch. The main yarn will appear on the front of the stitch and the secondary on its back.

Pointelle, in knitting: same as **knitted lace.** An openwork knitting structure. Openings are created by transferring stitches to one of the neighboring needles and picking up a new stitch on the emptied needle. In hand knitting, it is a combination of decreases (two stitches knitted or purled together) and eyelets (yarn over).

Primary color: any of a group of colors from which all other colors can be obtained by mixing.

PTS, or **Power Tension Setting:** Stoll technology that allows for different stitch length assignment for any individual stitch within the same row of knitting.

Plush: a rich fabric of silk, cotton, wool, or a combination of these fibers, with a long, soft nap.

Quilt or **quilted:** a textile made of two layers of cloth filled with padding (batting) held in place by lines of stitching.

Running stitch, in hand sewing and embroidery: the stitch is worked by passing the needle in and out of the fabric at a regular distance. Straight or running stitch is the basic stitch on which all other forms of sewing are based.

Secondary color: a color resulting from the mixing of two primary colors.

Single-bed structure: a knitting structure that uses needles on only one bed at a time.

Single jersey: also known as **stockinette** or **stocking stitch.** Plain fabric knitted on single bed with knit stitches appearing on its face and purl on its reverse.

Stitch density, in knitting: same as **tension.** The number of knitted rows (courses) and stitches (columns) in a knitted fabric counted within a square of a given size, usually 10 cm x 10 cm (4" x 4"), 1" x 1", or 1 cm x 1 cm.

Stitch length, in knitting: same as **stitch size.** The size of the stitch is determined by the amount of yarn that went into making it, which is in turn determined by the needle position (NP) during the forming of the stitch. For Stoll users also known as **NP value.**

Structure-independent color effects: in this text, same as **technology-based color effect,** the color effect created by use of a specific knitting technique or technology, such as plating.

Torquing, in knitting: also known as **biasing,** a common occurrence in fabric knitted with a single-ply yarn. Fabrics knitted on a single needle bed, like single jersey, will bias.

Unbalanced: in this text, related to knitting structure. Structure will be considered unbalanced if its front bed row count differs from its back bed row count. Number of rows created on a face of a fabric are different from the number of rows created on its back.

V (Needle) Bed, in knitting: same as **double-bed.** A knitting machine with two needle beds, front and rear (back), which are arranged in an inverted "V" shape. This arrangement allows for the transfer of stitches from one bed to the other, as well as knitting tubular and double-bed (knit and purl) structures.

Warp, in weaving: the vertical threads on a loom over and under which other threads (the weft) are passed to make a cloth.

Weft, in weaving: the crosswise threads passed over and under warp threads on a loom to make a cloth.

Yarn feeder, in knitting: same as **yarn carrier.** The part of a knitting machine that has a yarn threaded into it to be laid into a needle to form a stitch, to tuck or to float. The feeder is picked up and moved by a carriage. The new generation of machines, such as Stoll ADF, have motorized yarn feeders that can move independently of a carriage.

Yarn carrier, in knitting: same as **yarn feeder.**

About the Authors

Jörg Hartmann is a fashion designer and, since
2002, has served as Head of Fashion & Technology
at KARL MAYER STOLL. He is also a Professor
of Knitwear Design at the Staatliche Akademie
der Bildenden Künste in Stuttgart. Additionally,
Jörg has designed his own label of knitwear and
worked as a creative consultant to a number of
notable fashion brands. He is committed to sharing his experience, knowledge, and passion
with others.

Anna Gitelson-Kahn is an Associate Professor
and the Graduate Program Director of the Textiles Department at the Rhode Island School
of Design. She has extensive experience in the
field of knitting and has previously designed knits
for interiors under her own label. Anna is passion-
ate about teaching and sharing her knowledge
with the next generation of artists and designers.
She brings her teaching expertise to this book,
to make its content accessible to experienced
and novice audiences alike.

Luca Missoni has directed knitwear research
and product development, and designed men's
and sport collections for the brand founded by
his parents, Ottavio and Rita Missoni. Today, he
is Artistic Director of the Missoni Archive, which
he developed as a research tool and a communication project to enhance the historical and
artistic heritage of the brand. He also curates
museum exhibitions and visual and performing
arts projects.

Image Directory

Arnoldsche Art Publishers would like to express their gratitude to the institutions and individuals who generously provided photographic material for use in this book. We have made every effort to identify the current copyright holders but apologize in advance for any unintentional omission or error. We will gladly include the appropriate acknowledgment in any future edition.

Please note that the picture credit only mentions the rights of external parties who participated in the shooting of previous STOLL Trend Collections. All other image rights belong to Karl Mayer Stoll Textilmaschinenfabrik GmbH.

Photography Trend Collection Color in Knitting by Antje Peters
p. 10, 2310001; p. 20, 2210023; p. 25, 2210019; p. 31, 2310002; p. 37, 2310006; p. 41, 2210029; p. 42, 2210034; p. 51, 2210039; p. 56, 2210027; p. 70, 2310004

Photography Trend Collection Wonderful by Rafael Krötz, Model: Nele N./Modelwerk
p. 21, 2110065; p. 66, 2110073

Photography Trend Collection Faster: From Concept to Store by Theresa Marx, Model: Une Jonynaite/M4
p. 47, 1910078; p. 48, 1910052; p. 91, 2010001

Photography Trend Collection Materialization by Roman Goebel, Models: Sofie Theobald/LeManagement, Anatol Modzelewski/M4
p. 13, 1810116; p. 52, 1810097; p. 55 1810118; p. 94, 1810104; p. 95, 1810090; p. 96 1810088; p. 99, 1810119; p. 100, 1910024; p. 102 1810124

Photography Trend Collection Skateboarding by Paolo Zerbini
p. 16, 1710036

Photography Trend Collection The Bike Messenger Collection by Roman Goebel, Model: Ben Smallwood/M4
p. 54, 1610056; p. 92, 1610053

Photography Trend Collection Performance Plus Collection by Amos Fricke, Model: Irene Amuquandho/Place
p. 74, 1610003

Photography Trend Collection ITMA 2015 Capsule Collection by Rafael Krötz/SSAW
p. 40, 1510102; p. 109, 1510077

Photography Trend Collection Woven Stitches by Roman Goebel, Model: Maria Port/Model Management
p. 18, 1510042; p. 34, 1510044; p. 69, 1510036

Photography Trend Collection Urban Natives by Roman Goebel, Model: Eloisa Birleanu/Modelwerk
p. 64, 1410134; p. 73, 1410097; p. 111, 1410117

Photography Trend Collection Denim by Rafael Krötz Model: Nele Kenzler/Place Models, Panagiotis Gianneas/Place Models
p. 84, 1210166; p. 85, 1210177; p. 86, 1310018

Photography Trend Collection Flamboyant by Rafael Krötz, Model: Thea Stratton/Next London
p. 38, 1210059; p. 58, 1210121; p. 62, 1210019

Design p. 59, 1210101 by Velia Dietz

Photography swatches by Max Siewert

Acknowl-edgments

Color in Knitting would not have been possible without the help of many people. We are especially grateful to following individuals for their contributions to this book and their dedication to the world of knitwear design.

First, our co-writers: we wish to express our gratitude to **Anna Gitelson-Kahn** for cowriting this book and bringing her extensive teaching experience to the project. And, a very special thank you goes to **Luca Missoni.** Who else would be better suited to write a testimonial on the interaction between color and knitting technique than he, given his connection to this topic due to his background, profession, and his artistic and technical skills in this field?

We would also like to thank **Heather A. McDonald** for her skillful copyediting, and **Thorsten Grimm** and **Oliver Moore** of SSAW Studio for their valuable contributions.

We also want to recognize our team members at Stoll Fashion & Technology, who contributed their knowledge, talents, and energy to this project: **Ellen Judith Müller,** designer, for her invaluable coordination and communication efforts; **Karen Klabunde,** designer, for her creative input in the book's concept phase; **Francesco Collura,** senior programmer, for his technical expertise; **Petra Meyer,** for her knowledge of yarns and colors; **Antonia di Toma,** for her finishing work; and our programmers **Yasmin Ereür, Gerold Frischke, Thomas Nonnenmacher, Achim Ulmer,** and **Sebastian Wandel,** for their contributions to the final selection of samples.

References

Françoise Tellier-Loumagne, **The Art of Knitting: Inspirational Stitches, Textures, and Surfaces,** Thames & Hudson Ltd., London, 2005

Sandy Black, **Knitwear in Fashion,** Thames & Hudson Inc., New York, 2005

Further Reading

Luciano Caramel, Luca Missoni, and Emma Zanella, eds., **Missoni: L'arte, il Colore,** Rizzoli editore, RCS Libri Spa, Milan, 2015

Sandy Black, **Knitting: Fashion, Industry, Craft,** V&A Publishing, London, 2012

Alison Ellen, **Knitting: Colour, Structure and Design,** The Crowood Press Ltd., Wiltshire, 2011

Lisa Donofrio-Ferrezza and Marilyn Hefferen, **Designing a Knitwear Collection,** Fairchild Books Inc., New York, 2008

Imprint

Editors
Jörg Hartmann, Anna Gitelson-Kahn

Authors
Jörg Hartmann, Anna Gitelson-Kahn, Luca Missoni

Concept and graphic design
ssawstudio.com

Translations
Jörg Hartmann, Anna Gitelson-Kahn, Luca Missoni

Copy editing
Heather A. McDonald

Printed by
Offizin Scheufele, Stuttgart

Paper
GardaMatt Art 150 g/qm, Tauro Natur 150 g/qm

Bibliographic information published by the Deutsche Nationalbibliothek

The Deutsche Nationalbibliothek lists this publication in the Deutsche Nationalbibliografie; detailed bibliographic data are available at www.dnb.de.

ISBN 978-3-89790-702-7

Made in Germany, 2023

Cover illustrations
front/back:
© Karl Mayer Stoll Textilmaschinenfabrik GmbH

This book has been produced with the generous support of
Karl Mayer Stoll Textilmaschinenfabrik GmbH

STOLL
by KARL MAYER